TESTIMONIALS

Sharkie Zartman has written a must read book for all of us aging athletes who refuse to give in and want to meet head on the challenges of growing older. As a former collegiate and professional athlete and now an orthopaedic surgeon and sports medicine specialist, I address these issues everyday not only with my own body but also those of my patients. Sharkie is right on with her approach to aging as a sport and tackles it with a proactive approach that will leave you grinning from ear to ear with each page of this great read. I urge all to read it and learn that winning the game of aging can be done with determination, strategy and grace."

Bill Stetson, MD
Stetson Powell Orthopaedics and Sports Medicine
Associate Clinical Professor, University of Southern California
Keck School of Medicine, Team Orthopaedic Surgeon, USA Men's and
Women's USA Volleyball Team

If you are a Baby Boomer like me and have been looking for a sensible strategy to win at the sport of "Aging" then the game plan Sharkie Zartman brings to the field in this book should be studied carefully like an opponent's film. Based on her training as a world class volleyball player and coach, her indomitable outlook on how to attack the symptoms and challenges of becoming older lays out simple guidelines that ensure you a sporting chance of retaining a full and vibrant life To quote her directly: "If you think you are old you will start to act like it and the body will follow." By comparing aging to the logistics, training and experiences she learned as a professional athlete, Sharkie compels you think about growing older as a sport where you connect with your inner athlete, meet your competition head on and beat old age at it's own game."

Jay Lickus
623.734.5438
www.survive55.com

Sharkie Zartman *Takes on Aging as a sport* ... as a former All'American volleyball Player who competed for UCLA, and was also a member of the USA National Team in 1974, Sharkie Zartman brings her experience as a former athlete and award winning coach to the pages of this thought provoking book. Sharkie Zartman learned from sorts and these valuable lessons and skills can easily be applied to the challenges of Aging. As a professor in the areas of health and fitness, she also brings her academic experience to this important subject. This is a book for Baby Boomers as they develop their life plan regarding Health and Wellness.

Rick Bava Author of "In Search of the Baby Boomer Generation"

Take on Aging as a sport brings real advice, real understanding, real purpose to a very real challenge: aging. Sharkie Zartman has a talent for teaching while keeping you interested. If you wish to grow old with pep in your step, I strongly suggest you read this book.

The Brain Broad—Lynette Louise, Internationally renowned
neurotherapist, author, speaker, producer, host
and proud mother to eight miraculous children.

Highly readable, motivating, encouraging, and helping the reader to accept themselves and move forward to greater health and enjoyment.

Brian Weatherdon, certified financial planner and
retirement coach and author of "A Lifetime of Wealth."

Sharkie nails it in this amazing book on the aging process. Getting older doesn't have to be a bad thing, and this book proves just that!

Cornell Thomas, author, "The Power of Positivity" and "The Power Of Me"

Sharkie Zartman's new book appeals to me because I'm right in line with her thinking. At age 60, I reunited our rock 'n roll band "The Invictas." During the 60's we had thousands of fans due to our record and dance called "The Hump." Since reuniting in 2005, we've been featured on NBC's Today Show, in USA Today, played with The Beach Boys and we're rocking thousands of boomers with our high energy classic rock show. None of us on stage are young guys, we're all 60 plus. As Sharkie says in her book, *Take on Aging as a Sport,* we are all aging and every part of our body and mind is vulnerable to aging. I believe her book will help inspire millions of us who refuse to go down without a fight. At age 72, I run around on stage like a kid, my job is not only to entertain, I want to inspire others to follow their dreams and live life to the fullest. I am with you 100% and her book that will inspire me to continue doing what I'm doing because "I refuse to grow up." We call our concept "Rock Till Ya Drop." And I'm going to keep Sharkie's book close to me at all times.

Herb Gross
www.theinvictas.com

TAKE ON
AGING AS A
SPORT

THE ATHLETIC APPROACH TO AGING

SHARKIE ZARTMAN

Published by Motivational Press, Inc.
1777 Aurora Road
Melbourne, Florida, 32935
www.MotivationalPress.com

Manufactured in the United States of America.

ISBN: 978-1-62865-299-4

CONTENTS

PREFACE

SHARKIE IS AN AMAZING PERSON. I AM SO LUCKY TO HAVE HER IN MY life as my wife of forty years and I am honored to write the preface to this wonderful book for her.

As an author, Sharkie is unique in the range and subject matter of her books. She has written books on Fitness, Wellness, Yoga, Volleyball Coaching and Empowerment.

Take On Aging as a Sport, her newest book, is both timely and timeless. Everyone has "Aged," is "Aging" and will "Age." In today's world, we have extended length of life, but have not adequately addressed quality of life. This has created apprehension, fear, and uncertainty regarding such things as illness and pain, Alzheimer's and dementia, and coping and functioning as we Age.

The good news is that these issues are not out of our hands and uncontrollable. Attitude is important; how you feel about Aging is important. It is important to accept and embrace the aging process, both its ups and downs. Our bodies are designed to serve us throughout our entire lives. Thus we should expect to be vital and energized, to have the ability to overcome and resist, and to maximize every day of our lives.

We should remember the old Adage: "Use It or Lose It," and apply that to both body and mind. We should find ways to be active and useful, to be independent and respected, and to expect to have a long, fulfilling, productive, and healthy life. Be Too Fit To Die; Don't Go Easy!

Take Sharkie's book to heart. Learn from the wealth of information that she gives to you. Glom onto the insights and game plans that she presents to you. AND, Take On Aging As a Sport

Pat Zartman

FOREWORD

I AM HONORED TO PRESENT A COMMENTARY ON THIS BOOK *TAKE ON AGING as a Sport---The Athletic Approach to Aging* by Sharkie Zartman. My area of expertise is to chronicle the Baby Boomer Generation. At the heart of Baby Boomers in the 21st century is Health and Wellness. Three things come to my attention on this subject: mind, body, and spirit. With this comes the tutorial from Sharkie Zartman, who brings her expertise to a subject that is of great importance: Aging and Aging Well.

As a former All-American volleyball player who competed for UCLA, Sharkie Zartman was also a member of the USA National team in 1974. I would like to think of the book as a game plan for the Health and Wellness of Baby Boomers. Sharkie learned valuable lessons from sports that she applied to this book, and as a professor in the areas of health and fitness, she also brings her academic experience to this subject. This is a book for Baby Boomers as they develop a path forward regarding Health and Wellness.

It is hard to believe that the generation who once uttered the phrase, "don't trust anyone over thirty," is now thinking about the skill set for aging well. But the time has come for Baby Boomers to establish a game plan for their life, no different than John Wooden once did for the award willing teams of UCLA Basketball. That is the secret to Sharkie Zartman's book, for she provides practical council on the use of sports that goes beyond a metaphor. Think of Sharkie as the coach and you, the reader, as the player on her team as she walks you through the mental and physical aspects of aging and the use of sports as a tool for your success.

The thesis of this book and the recommendation of Sharkie Zartman are that you must stay active. Yes, a strong body built by activity will also make your brain stronger. Baby Boomers, many of them grandparents, are not their grandparents—grandparent. The Baby Boomer of the here and now does not want to just sit on the porch, rocking their grandchildren, for they want to continue to rock the world. Baby Boomers are young at heart, and Sharkie's principles are designed to match reality with attitude. For as she articulates, the lessons learned from athletic competition can be applied to the development of a rich and long life.

Baby Boomers are optimistic about the future; they expect to live a long life. But to make that happen, one needs more than medical science. They need to eat well, exercise, and stay active. A long life does not just happen, you need to work at it, and with the help of Sharkie's Zartman's play book, the aging process can be fun. We as Baby Boomers are sports enthusiasts. We still follow our favorite teams, why not apply the acumen of Sharkie Zartman, to our own championship team?

So in conclusion, let me say the Baby Boomer who has read, or will read this book, will find lessons, council and coaching to the greatest game of all, the game of life!

Rick Bava author of "In Search of the Baby Boomers"

This book is dedicated to my amazing Dad, Leonard Boehnert, who as a person in his ninth decade of life is still one of the most vibrant people I know. He appreciates each and every day, and whenever I see him or talk to him, he always greets me with a "Hi Ya!" I am so proud to be his daughter and have appreciated all of his advice throughout my life. My favorite "daddyisms" have been: "Always try your best; you can't do any better than your best" and "Slow down and smell the bees" and "Every day above the ground is a good day."

I love him with all my heart!

INTRODUCTION

W HEN I WAS A KID, THE LAST THING I WANTED TO DO WAS GET OLD. When you're young you don't care about how long you live. You just want to have fun and for the most part, live day-to-day, moment-by-moment.

Most of the older people I knew back then were crotchety, complained a lot, dressed funny, and seemed like they weren't enjoying life at all. What appeared to make them happy was making everyone else miserable. The only exception to the rule was my Granddad, who even though he looked his age, never acted like it. He always had a twinkle in his eye, a spring in his step, was active and seemed to love life and everyone around him.

Even so, when I was 13 years old my friend and I did some research on the OUIJA board and I asked the scariest question I could think of: When was I going to die? The board answered 28 years old. I remember being fine with that since it seemed so far away.

However, now that I have lived long past 28 years, I have to tell you, life has been a fun, wild, challenging ride and I don't intend to settle for any less just because I have officially reached senior citizen status. On the contrary, I think the second half of life is when we need to really go for it. After all, what are we waiting for? It really can be a great time in our lives, and even the best time if we can finally learn to make our health and happiness a priority, instead of going after money and fame and trying to please everyone but ourselves. We can even go back to how it was when we were children——having fun, living day-by-day, moment-by-moment.

And it's not just me who thinks this. Researchers and scientists are now discovering that how we feel about our age matters. If we focus on the negative aspects of aging in terms of decline or disability, our health will suffer as a result. In fact, the recent Baltimore Longitudinal Study of Aging suggests that people who were inclined to believe that older individuals were slower, unhappier and less sharp than the rest of us are more likely when they become older themselves to exhibit brain changes seen in those with Alzheimer's disease.[1]

How's that for motivating us to change our negative views of aging?

However, if we view aging with a positive mindset, take a proactive approach and take charge of our health and continue to seek opportunities for growth, our bodies will respond positively. The mind-body connection can become either our best ally or our worst enemy as we age.

I am not a doctor, so please don't think I have the latest pill, the best lifestyle advice, or can save anyone from himself or herself. I don't have a perfect body or perfect skin and I have my own challenges with the aging process.

However, I have taught health at the college level for forty years, have competed at the highest level in my sport, and have coached athletes of all ages and levels. I definitely have a unique perspective on how to navigate the unpredictable waters of aging in the 21st century, and I want to share it with you in this book.

What I know for sure is that we are all different and none of us ages the same. Don't you know people in their twenties and thirties who act like they are sick and tired of life and people in their eighties and nineties who are joyful, loving and exciting to be around? I think being different is one of our greatest assets.

My Dad named me after a killer fish, so I was always kind of an odd-ball growing up. But to be truthful, I really didn't want to be like everyone else and I certainly don't want to follow the crowd that thinks you should act your age. I've never been this age before. How am I supposed to act? Why can't I just enjoy life as best as I can?

As a young girl, I loved playing sports and was considered to be a Tomboy. Isn't it funny that we called girls who played sports "Tomboys" back then? Volleyball was my sport and I had high aspirations, wanting to compete in college and even wear a USA uniform and compete for my country. It took seven years and intense training and dedication to reach my goals, and I know that I developed a lot of wonderful physical and mental skills from playing my sport through the years that have helped me in many areas of my life. Now that I am in my sixties, I can still connect with my inner athlete, even though I no longer play volleyball because according to my doctor, the insides of my knees look like a war zone.

So, no, I didn't want to get old, but now that I'm here, I realize that you don't have to suffer many of the effects of aging if you take it on like a sport. Winning at sports does not come easily and takes work, both physically and mentally, to prepare for success.

Winning at aging takes the same work in order to have a fun, fulfilled life, no matter what the calendar says. And I think that should be our focus. I don't want to be one of those people that I knew when I was young who had given up on life and were grumpy and no fun to be around.

So I'm ready to stand up to aging and to train for a better quality of life until the end. I don't want any regrets that I didn't live my life to the fullest. It has been said that on our deathbeds, we are not going to be that concerned about what we did in our lives—we will be more concerned about lost opportunities and not doing things that we wanted. So, are you ready to play the most important sport of your life? Let's go for it!

CHAPTER ONE

THE ATHLETIC APPROACH TO AGING

"The spirit, the will to win and the will to excel---these are the things that endure and these are the qualities that are so much more important than any of the event that occasion them."

—*Vincent Lombardi*

CHANCES ARE, YOU PROBABLY PLAYED A SPORT SOMETIME IN YOUR life whether it was recreational or competitive and learned a ton from that experience. Even if you never played a sport, I'll bet you have watched at least a few and enjoyed the competition and even dreamed about being out there yourself!

Well, guess what? The most demanding sport is one that all of us who make it past fifty will play whether we want to or not and it's recruiting you now. Just wait, the next time you go to your doctor and ask what's wrong and he looks at you with a smirk and says the word we all hate to hear....

The word is *Aging*.

The Sport of Aging has many rules, strategies, techniques, demands, and above all, is ruthless. It never stops challenging us in ways we have never experienced before. The good news is that even though we cannot stop the process of aging, we can control *how* we age. We all want to live a life that is fulfilling, rewarding and fun for as long as possible.

However, in order to do so, we need to activate our inner athlete, step up to the challenges and change our near-sighted views of aging.

As athletes, we cannot and will not accept the current paradigm in our country that believes aging is mostly about decline. On the contrary, aging is about challenge, taking charge of our lives and no longer taking our days for granted. It's an honor to get to play the game! Just look at all the people we know who didn't make it this far.

So the choice is ours: Are we going to let aging beat us up or are we going to learn how to play the game?

Obviously we will not be able to control everything that we come up against in the aging game, just like we couldn't control every challenge and obstacle we encountered in our sport, but we can TAKE CHARGE and that's what taking on aging as a sport is all about. Also, it's never too late to get into the game. You can start playing at any age; however, this is a game that you never want to quit.

To win at the sport of aging does not mean to live forever and I'm not sure anyone would really want that. My husband, Pat, claims that he is going to live to be 200 because he wants to beat the Russian that supposedly lived to be 175 years old.

Seriously?

I told him that he might need to get another wife or two, or three. I have no desire to join him on his competitive, patriotic journey.

Even though we might not make it to 200, winning at aging is possible if we have the right perspective. What we want is to be functional and comfortable in our bodies as we get up in years. We want to stay emotionally healthy and for our minds and memories to remain sharp. We want to be valued and capable of helping others and sharing our talents. We want to feel loved, valuable and needed at any age.

What we don't want is to live long and be a burden on others, suffer a long period of decline, not able to enjoy our final years or help others. Also, as Roger Landry so eloquently states in the title of his incredible book, we basically want to *Live Long and Die Short*.[1]

So how do we play the game? If you ever played a sport in your life, you needed to know the rules, learn the techniques, and get your body in shape to participate, eat to fuel performance, learn strategies, get your mind on board, and scout your opponents. Perhaps all your training has prepared you for how you will deal with the most insidious sport of all, The Sport of Aging.

Are you ready?

The first thing that any athlete learns about the sport is the rules. Aging has a few rules that don't change. Here are some of them:

1. Everything living thing ages. It is a normal part of our existence.

2. Every part of the body and mind is vulnerable to aging.

3. You can live a healthy, fulfilling life at any age.

4. You are responsible for how you handle the aging process. Doctors can only do so much.

5. The rate of aging is related to lifestyle, attitude and genetics, and we can control two out of those three!

6. Physiological and psychological conditions are more powerful than chronological age.

7. People do not age at the same rate or have the same conditions. It is an individualized process.

8. When it comes to winning at the game of aging, it doesn't matter who you are—it matters what you do.

9. Aging is a bitch. Respect, study, and understand the beast, or she will take away your quality of life.

10. How we age is ultimately up to us. We are in the driver's seat if we would just get behind the wheel and stop being a passenger or a back-seat driver.

Before we start understanding how to play the sport of aging, believe it or not, there are perks to getting older. If you remember playing your sport, there were hard, challenging times, but there were also amazing fun times that we all cherished. And those experiences were worth the challenge and the hard work.

Here are some perks of aging that most of us will experience and will help keep us motivated when the going gets tough.

1. People over 50 tend to be happier that their younger counterparts.

2. As we age, we tend to live more in the present moment rather than obsessing about the future. We don't care to think about where we will be in 10, 20, 30 years.

3. We no longer care what people think and stop trying to please others. If I want to paint my nails all different colors or wear my shirts inside out, so be it.

4. We have more time to finally figure out what we want to do instead of what other people want us to do.

5. We appreciate life and enjoy things we never even noticed before when we were young and too busy.

6. We have life experience that guides us in making important decisions and we are great resources to others. In other words, we are wiser because we have been there and done that.

7. We no longer have to raise our children. In fact, they'd better be nice to us if they want any money when we move on.

8. If we are lucky enough to have grandchildren, we can love them, play with them, spoil them, and give them back.

9. We can have more fun and not be concerned about looking immature. We already grew up and now we can be like a kid again!

10. Seniors get great discounts.

11. If you take care of yourself, you won't look your age and will be happy to shock people when they ask you how old you are. Be proud of your age. My dad is the poster child for 91 years young.

The Game of Aging has many levels and types of opponents. If you are younger than 50, you have been competing in the Pony League---the one for beginners, and you have probably been successful in not letting age interfere with what you want to do. After 50, you get to move up a division---and this is when it starts to get competitive. After 60, the competition is fierce and ready to kick your butt every time you wake up. 70 and above, you hit the Master's Division, and can teach us youngins a thing or two.

Someone once said: "Aging is NOT for Sissies." I always thought that phrase was meaningless and degrading until recently. Is it just me or does our body sometimes takes on a mind of its own and not work like it used to? Why all of the sudden am I limping, or can't move one of my fingers, or just acquired four more wrinkles overnight? Who came into my room in the middle of the night when I was asleep and beat me up? Where did these bruises come from? I don't remember falling or getting hit.

And the surprises just keep on coming!

THE POWER OF RAP

As a competitor in the Sport of Aging, besides physical training, you must get your mind on board. Three of the characteristics you probably used to be successful in your sport will be more important than ever as you move through the years. They are resiliency, accountability and the power of purpose.

In the aging game, we have to be ready for anything and everything and let nothing set us back from living fully, When you were a young athlete, you probably got beat up a lot, and lost some important games. Did you whine and moan or quit?

When we get knocked down by one of age's bombs, we have to brush it off, get back up and keep moving forward. In other words, we have to have resiliency. If we feel sorry for ourselves or don't take action, we'll get run over, become an aging statistic and end up being a grumpy old person no one wants to be around. Who, if anyone, wants to live like that? So it's time to thicken our skin and get tough! These speed bumps are part of the road we travel as we age. It's the price of being on this planet longer than our departed friends.

I once had an amazing friend named Diana. Our daughters were on a gymnastics team together and we used to sit in the stands and feel each other's pain and excitement as our daughter flew around uneven bars, did back flips on the balance beam, and hurled their bodies over a vault. We shared a lot of joy, excitement, and sheer terror. A while back, Diana was diagnosed with breast cancer, had surgery, rounds of chemotherapy, and went back to her teaching job and raising her five beautiful children. Unfortunately, five years later, the cancer came back for a second round and this time had spread to her bones and she was told the cancer had progressed to stage four. Diana made a decision she was not going to give up and went on chemo again, and endured extreme fatigue and nausea—the common side effects of the treatment. She bought a stylish wig to cover up her bald head and continued to work full time, focusing on her first grade students. She didn't want sympathy——what she wanted was to continue to make a difference and enjoy whatever time she had left.

She also decided that it was time to do some serious traveling. Diana and her husband started to travel all around the world and we were lucky enough to go with them to the Caribbean. We had so much fun it was hard to believe that my friend was so sick. We lived like there was no tomorrow, and spent every day at the spa, danced every night, drank the most expensive wine, went on excursions and gambled to our heart's content. I spent so much money that it took me three years to pay for the trip, but it was worth every penny.

Diana never complained about her condition. Instead she used it as a reason to enjoy life to the fullest and be thankful for each and every new day. None of her colleagues or students knew that she was battling cancer. When she listened to their problems, she would just smile, offer advice and sometimes gently shake her head. If they only knew the truth I'm sure they would have felt silly about telling her their trivial problems while she was battling a killer disease. My friend found the upside of being diagnosed with a deadly disease. Instead of feeling sorry for herself, she opened up, embraced life, and found a new purpose in being an incredible example for her friends and family. She fought her cancer with dignity and grace and left an incredible legacy when she finally passed away.

Shortly after Diana's passing, one of my students came up to me after class and started playing the whining game—complaining about school, her family, her health and anything else she thought would get a sympathetic ear. She was a mess and I wasn't in the mood to listen. Finally I said, "If you stop complaining about your life, maybe it will get better." She stopped cold, gave me a look of shock, and then slowly walked away. At first I felt bad coming down on her so hard, but she never used me as a dumping ground anymore for her problems, and I think she might have toughened up a little——at least when she was around me.

Winning at the game of aging is tough and not for wimps. And athletes are not wimps! We are better than that! As we play the aging game we need to remember that winning is an ongoing process. We win some bouts, and we lose some, but we never give up on life! If you saw the Rocky movies, you know that this was the major theme and one reason why they became such hits. Rocky was always getting knocked down, but he never stayed down, much to his opponent's surprise. So what's it going to be? Life is too precious and there is still so much more to enjoy, experience, and share. So toughen up and enjoy the bumpy ride!

Another important area that all athletes are aware of is Accountability. If we made a mistake, instead of blaming it on our teammates, officials or coaches, we took responsibility for our actions and worked on our weaknesses so they wouldn't cost us the next game.

However, if you are like me, you probably did some irresponsible things when you were younger, and somehow got away with them. For example: partying all night with friends, and the next day competing in your sport. At the time, it was no big deal and even fun to brag about. It seemed that we were invincible and didn't realize that our lifestyle would eventually catch up to us. Now that we are in the aging game, those days are over! If we don't get a full night's sleep, or have one too many drinks, the next day is down-right painful.

Welcome to being accountable for your actions all the time!

Unfortunately, these days, blaming or expecting others to fix us is an epidemic. But, unless you accept the responsibility for your choices, you will never have any power over your life, and you will definitely lose many of the aging battles.

I remember going to a workshop for trainers a while back, and one of the topics was helping people to lose weight. There were several speakers, who all professed to have the latest pill or gimmick guaranteed to shed the pounds. I remember one product where you wore a belt around your waist that contracted your abdominal muscles for you---it was like doing over 300 sit-ups. Another was a pill where most of the fat that a person ate was not absorbed into the system. A popular item, except when you found out that intestinal incompetence was a side effect...in other words, pooping in your pants.

One person got up and announced that he didn't have a pill or a product, but he did have something that worked. He said to have your clients stand in front of a mirror without any clothes by themselves, look into their own eyes and say, "I am responsible for this, and I am the only one who can fix it."

Needless to say, he wasn't very popular. In fact, I think a lot of the people in the audience threw their sample protein bars at him. However, his message was the best. If we want to have success in our lives, we have to be responsible for our actions. When it comes to having a vibrant, fulfilled life as we age, *we are the ones in charge.* Doctors are helpful in dealing with disease states, but they do not make our choices for us... so if we screw up, it's on us.

As an athlete, you knew that once you were in the game, the coach could only do so much. He or she didn't contact the ball or make on the court decisions. The only way that you could improve your game was by looking at your strengths and especially your weaknesses and making sure you addressed them. If you lost a competition, if wasn't your coaches' fault, your teammates' fault or the conditions. If you focused on that, you would have never gotten good at your sport, because as you knew back then, you can't control these outside forces.

And so it is with the Aging Game. All you can do is control yourself, your choices and your attitudes.

So how can you be accountable with the aging process? First, look at the choices that got you where you are today. None of us look like we did when we were twenty, unless we have had so much cosmetic surgery that our belly button in now on top of our heads. If we do have a doctor that is helping us through a medical challenge, we must trust him or her and also do our part in following directions and taking responsibility for the seemingly simple things, like getting enough sleep, drinking enough water, eating whole foods, and getting exercise in our lives.

Finally, every athlete who is successful knows about the Power of Purpose. Purpose is hard to define, but obvious when people have it. Regardless of age, they are usually happier, healthier, and look forward to each day. They are stable, and when life gets tough, instead of giving up, they use their assurance of purpose as an anchor to make it through the tough times. In other words, they know what they want and are driven to get it.

It's also obvious when people have not yet discovered it, they tend to be bored, tired all the time, depressed, and dissatisfied with life. Even if you are doing what you are good at, and are successful, if you don't like it, you are not "on purpose."

A purposeful life means being in your element. Your purpose is a deep treasure buried inside of you, just waiting to be discovered. And the good news is that you can discover it anytime you want.

So why don't we all know our purpose? Aren't we taught to seek it out?

Not really.

We are trained and educated to think that the purpose of life equals social status, establishing a career, accumulating wealth, winning, and being powerful and popular. I'm sure you know people who appear to have it all, but who are incredibly unhappy and don't know why.

Another negative influence is social norming----- a part of childhood where you learn how to act in relation to everyone else. Getting grades, doing what is expected, and following set standards are all examples of social norming. This usually is not a problem unless it interferes with people discovering their unique talents and gifts. Unfortunately, some of these are not always nurtured as we are growing up and ultimately become smothered.

So what does it take to discover our own purpose? First, we must get quiet and move our awareness inside. Then, ask yourself these questions, each and every day:

1. Why am I alive today?

2. How can I serve?

3 What do I really want in my life?

4. What are my innate strengths?

5. What do I enjoy doing the most that makes me come alive?

5. Where can I add the greatest value?

Having a sense of purpose promotes physical, mental and spiritual health. People who live their life with purpose are usually healthier, happier and live longer. Purpose is what inspires you to get up in the morning!

Many people who have retired feel that they have lost their sense of value because they are no longer working at a job. But you don't need a job to make a difference. One of the positive perks about getting older is you can finally take the time to discover what it is that you really love and how you can make the world a better place.

So isn't it worth spending some time to discover your purpose? Don't be a person that is smothered by expectations, life demands, or just stuck in survival mode. You are so much better than that!

Now is the time to gravitate towards things that inspire you and make you feel more alive! Start living your life on purpose and watch your life change. I promise you will notice a huge difference!

I want to share with you a poem written by a fellow author, and friend, Don Hurzeler. He is a retired CEO/President of Zurich Middle Markets Insurance Company and a former president of the Zurich Foundation. He is now retired and living an amazing life in Hawaii, swimming and diving with sharks and taking the most amazing photographs for his new book. He never had the time to do these things when he was working in corporate America, and now, in his late sixties, Don is more vibrant and happy than ever. I love this poem he wrote in his book, *Designated for Success*.[2] I think it describes the challenges of not only life but also dealing with aging, and emphasizes the mindset necessary to win at life:

THE WINNER IN WAITING

Are you beaten down by life

Have you lost another race

Were you second at the finish

Has life slapped you in the face?

Is the world around you saying

That you're just not good enough

That someone does it better
That you just don't have the stuff?

I've got news for you my buddy
Let me tell you what I know
I'm aware of all your talents
This defeat is but a blow.

So get up off the canvas
Don't be jealous, don't be mad
Focus once again on winning
Victory's out there to be had.

The loss comes only
When you give up the fight
When you agree to be a loser
When you finally say "They're right"

You are a winner now in waiting
First prize will come, my friend
Work hard and you will get it
The only question's "When?"

They don't know you like I do
You're a winner, don't forget it
The next champion will be you!

Remember, we are all here for a purpose, and since we are still alive, we still have time to find our purpose, make a difference and leave our legacy. No one can interfere with what we are here to do. And that is what it really means to be a champion.

Are you ready to meet your competition?

CHAPTER TWO

MEET YOUR COMPETITION

"You never win a game unless you beat the guy in front of you. The score on the board doesn't mean a thing. That's for the fans. You've got to win the war with the man in front of you. You've got to get your man."

—*Vincent Lombardi*

I REMEMBER GOING TO MY OB-GYN A WHILE BACK AND WAS SHARING with my doctor various symptoms I had been experiencing that were interfering with my work performance. My energy had hit rock bottom, I was feeling more irritable than usual and even though I was exercising for over four hours a day teaching fitness classes at the college, I had developed an unsightly roll in my lower abdominal area. My doctor looked at my chart, and I assume my age, and then shook his head and said, "All these are complaints common for your age. Just slow down and accept where you are now."

"And the roll?"

"No exercise will get rid of that. It's common for women your age." Then he wrote me a prescription for Xanax and told me to call him right away if I had suicidal thoughts.

I remember coming out of that appointment feeling defeated and upset. I was in my mid-forties— if I felt like this now, what was coming ahead? I immediately decided to take action, and at least get rid of the roll. Yes, I had liposuction and had that fat sucked out. I didn't realize that it would hurt like hell afterward and was so swollen following the procedure, I looked worse for the next three weeks. One of my students even asked me if I was pregnant. And to make it worse, I was told that fat would never deposit there again since the fat cells were gone for good. What I wasn't told was that the fat would look for a new home, and the next most convenient place was my butt.

I made a promise to myself that day. First of all, that I would not resort to this type of surgery ever again, and that I would not let my age interfere with my quality of life. Just because my doctor was ready to drop me off at the curb because I was no longer fertile, didn't mean I was ready to give up on life. I was a competitor. What else did I have coming at me? I needed to prepare.

And by the way, I never took the Xanax.

All athletes size up their competition and realize that there are some easy challenges, moderate ones, and the heavy hitters. We often compete against the same teams and athletes from time to time, and sometimes win the match or event, and sometimes lose. But that doesn't mean we stop playing the game. We keep going back for more, and in the Sport of Aging, the competition just keeps getting fiercer. See why we need to activate our inner athletes? Getting older is not a negative thing, it's a privilege and in order to stay alive and thrive, we need to step up to the plate and take charge of our health and life. We are no longer coasting like we did when we were young.

So what's your competition?

These are the most common symptoms of aging and the good news is that these can be treated and even reversed with lifestyle changes and a little help from our medical team.

Eyesight Changes: Most people's eyesight changes as they age so this is probably the most common symptom most of us will encounter.

The good news is that we obviously have corrective lenses, contacts and even laser surgery. For those who are older, macular degeneration is also a common problem that can be corrected by a specialist who is trained in treatment options.

I remember when I finally decided that I needed glasses. I handed in my grades at the college wrong because I couldn't see the names clearly. What a mess to change all those grades just because I was too stubborn to admit that I needed glasses. Now, I love my glasses and look forward to trying different frames, transitional lenses and progressives. Now with so many options, don't delay if your sight is starting to be compromised.

Hearing Difficulties: Another common sign of aging is hearing loss, and is sometimes caused by loud noises, like loud rock music when we were young, infections, or genetics. My family has a condition called nerve deafness that does affect some of us as we age. I never wanted to get hearing aids, but I teach a lecture class at the college, and when I started answering questions I thought I heard that weren't even close, especially during the unit on sexuality, I finally decided that I needed some hearing aids.

It took a while to find ones that fit comfortably, and had a clear sound. I don't wear them all the time; because to tell you the truth, there are times that I just don't want to hear everything. My husband never knows when I have them on, so he doesn't know if I can't hear him or am just not listening to him. My family says that I should write a book entitled, *Do You Hear What I Hear?* Trust me, some of the things we thought we heard have been hilarious. For example, a while back I was shopping with my young daughter at a retail store, and she tugged at my shirt, and said, "Mommy, I don't like this section." Well, I heard it differently and told her: "Oh Sweetie, you don't need Liposuction."

Wrinkled Skin: Especially for women, this symptom causes a lot of anguish, because we tend to care about our looks, and each and every wrinkle gets our attention. Some people are blessed with beautiful skin and have taken great care of it by either staying out of the sun or using sunscreen religiously, and also have a great skin care routine. I was raised in Southern California and spent a lot of time at the beach. My skincare routine was putting baby and coconut oil on my skin to get a good tan—or should I say, sunburn. Little did I know how much damage I was doing at the time.

Today, we are much smarter, but for people like me, we need extra help. There are so many wonderful options available today. I've tried many of them and see a dermatologist regularly who brings his freeze gun when I come to his office to remove whatever new growth has blossomed on my skin. This is a lifetime process, but after all the time I spent in the sun in my youth, I'm lucky to still have my skin!

Senior Moments: Okay, these are scary. With the huge increase in dementia and Alzheimer's, whenever we have one of these incidents, we tend to think we are losing it. But there are perfectly normal reasons for us to temporarily lose our memory. For one thing, we usually have a lot of different things on our mind and the brain likes to focus on one thing at a time to be efficient. So if you can't find your purse in the car and notice that it's on the hood, or you can't find your sunglasses and they are on top of your head, don't panic. That's normal. Just try to slow down and stop multitasking. Senior moments are our brains' way of saying, "slow down, you're moving way too fast." I just saw a woman at the gym the other day who was working out on the elliptical machine, reading a book, listening to music and texting.

Seriously?

The following symptoms and conditions are your moderate competition and can be reversed, but will usually take more effort on your part. However, these are not serious unless you totally ignore them.

Fatigue: It seems these days that many people struggle with fatigue and there are many causes. As we get older, fatigue can become more problematic and even interfere with the quality of life, because we just don't have the energy to live our lives to the fullest. Fatigue sometimes can be alleviated by proper nutrition and in some instances, medication. However, one of the biggest causes of fatigue is stress, so it makes sense to have stress relievers on hand. The chapter, Time Out, has excellent suggestions on how to relieve stress and tune out the chaos.

Weight Gain: It's so unfair! As we age we actually need less food than we did in our 20's and thirties. Why? Because we lose muscle mass as we age if we don't exercise, and muscle burns a lot of calories. So if we lose muscle-burning power, those calories we take in get turned into—you guessed it——fat. Hormones also influence weight gain and with the hormone levels starting to diminish in our forties, for some people, especially women, the weight comes on slowly and steadily and is difficult to get off unless we consciously change our life style.

Sexual Dysfunction: Well I don't know about you, but I think this one sucks. Just because we don't want to have any more children doesn't mean that we don't want to have sex. However, again because of hormone decline, some people lose their sexual desire, some can't perform, or sex hurts instead of feels good. Hormonal replacement regimens including bioidenticals can help, but so can proper nutrition and exercise.

Arthritis: This condition is like an opponent that just keeps showing up and refuses to go away. If you come up against arthritis, chances are it will be a lifetime battle. Arthritis can appear in any joint in the body and causes swelling, pain and decreased range of motion. The joints that are the most problematic are the weight bearing joints—the hips and the knees.

Many people suffer for years, on and off and some resort to knee or hip replacement surgeries, although there are many other less invasive treatments available. Since we are all different in terms of the extent of the condition and our tolerances to discomfort, some treatments work for some and not others. Popular choices include glucosamine, injections, and physical therapy.

I tore the cartilage in my right knee at a mixed martial arts class, and didn't really think I had a severe injury until it became almost impossible to walk. Finally, I went to the doctor and he repaired the cartilage, but also noticed that I had some arthritis in my knee. I was shocked but not too concerned since I thought the surgery was all I needed.

Flash forward 20 years and two more surgeries. I think my left knee caught the arthritis from my right knee, although I know it isn't an infectious disease. If I wanted to replace any part of my body, instead of choosing a smaller butt, bigger breasts or a new face with perfect skin, I would sign up for new knees. At some point, I will probably have them both replaced, but I'm not ready yet. I would have to be crawling to choose a surgery that extensive.

Next are the heavy hitters. These diseases and conditions can be deadly and as we age, we are at higher risk. You don't want to take these lightly. If you are competing against one of these opponents, you really need to have an excellent medical support team, and also do your part in making your health and wellbeing THE priority in your life. The doctors cannot do it all. However, the best strategy is prevention with an active lifestyle, healthy eating, and seeing your doctor at least once a year for checkups. You want to avoid these opponents as much as possible.

HEART DISEASE

The MONSTER! This is the number one killer of both men and women in the westernized world. Age is a risk factor that we cannot change and so are genetics and medical history. However, there are more than twice as many risk factors we can control. And that is good news. The risks factors we can control are diabetes, stress, obesity, lack of activity, poor diet, smoking and inflammation. So if you have heart disease in your family or have been told that you have atherosclerosis, high blood pressure, or have suffered from angina, changing your lifestyle is no longer just a suggestion—-it's mandatory.

The symptoms of a heart attack include: anxiety; dizziness; sweating: sudden nausea: shortness of breath: unusual fatigue, pain, burning, squeezing, or pressure in chest; pain, numbness, pinching, or uncomfortable sensation in arms, back, jaw or neck. If you have any of these symptoms or someone you are with is having them, call 911 immediately. Time is of the essence. Don't mess with this monster. Even though my students are young at the college, I have them take a heart attack risk analysis from the Harvard School of Medicine. It's very easy to take and if you are at risk, it has excellent suggestions as to how to change your lifestyle and what you are doing that is putting you at the risk. Here is the link: www.diseaseriskindex.harvard.edu

CANCER: A BEAST WITH MANY FACES.

Half of all men and one third of all women will develop cancer in their lives. It is the second leading cause of death in the U.S with a 66% survival rate (for 5 years). Even though it is a serious disease, the good news is that most cancers are treatable if caught early. So that is our challenge. Not only to prevent it, but if we do get cancer, to catch it in its early stages.

So what is cancer? Cancer is a large group of diseases characterized by the uncontrolled growth and spread of abnormal cells. So it's not one disease, but several. What on earth causes cancer? I wish we had a clear-cut answer, but instead we have several theories that are probably all true to some extent, and when combined, increase the risk significantly.

Some of these include:

Carcinogens (food additives, tobacco, pollution, etc.)

Oncogenes (genetic predispositions)

Trauma or Stress

Radiation

Immune System Breakdown

Poor Nutrition

Viruses/Infections

Environmental Conditions

The most deadly cancers are lung cancer, colon cancer, breast cancer for women and prostate cancer for men, although cancer can occur most anywhere in the body. As we age, our risk of colon cancer, breast cancer and prostate cancer increases significantly, so it is very important to know the early warning signs. At the college, we teach the 7 early warning signs. These include:

Changes in the bowel or bladder; a sore that does not heal, unusual bleeding or discharge, thickening or lump in the breast or elsewhere; indigestion or difficulty in swallowing, obvious change in wart or mole, nagging cough or hoarseness.

What is interesting is that pain is not listed as an early warning sign, so if you don't go to the doctor unless something hurts really bad, you might end up being one of those people who gets cancer, but doesn't catch it until it is in the later stages, which is always more difficult to treat and cure.

Also, there are many other warning signs of cancer and I encourage people to be aware of any unusual sign that lasts for two weeks or more. Just get it checked out. Also, a great online resource is the American Cancer Society. They have all the latest information, specific warning signs and treatment options for every type of cancer. Check them out at www.cancer.org — especially if cancer runs in your family. Make sure you understand this beast and do everything you can to prevent it or catch it in its early stages.

DIABETES: THE SWEET DEVIL

Even though this disease can strike at any age, as we get up in years, it can show up when we least expect it. While not as deadly as heart disease or cancer, it is still very serious and can cause several health problems including amputations, blindness and put you at risk for heart disease. People mistakenly believe that you must be obese to be at risk, but that is not the case. While it's true that a lot of people who are obese also have diabetes, about half the people with diabetes have a normal body composition.

There are different types of diabetes, but the most common is Type II, which used to be called adult onset diabetes. However, we can't really call it that anymore because now we are seeing many children with the disease. So what's going on? Obviously, genetics are always a factor, but we need to look no further than our food supply to understand why we are seeing such a surge in this disease. Processed foods are high in sugar and low in fiber, and cause the body to secrete high amounts of insulin, the storage hormone. As this hormone stays elevated, the cells start to become resistant and then the blood sugar levels become dangerously high. One of the best things you can do to prevent diabetes is to clean up your diet. A great video from PBS that I highly recommend is called *Sweet Revenge with Dr. Lustig*. Trust me, it will shake you up and really make you rethink your food choices.

ALZHEIMER'S DISEASE; THE CRUELEST OPPONENT OF THEM ALL.

As we get up in years, one disease is waiting for approximately half of all of us who make it past 80. It's Alzheimer's Disease, which is probably the cruelest of all. It is a slow descent and robs a person of their cognitive abilities, their personality, memory, and ultimately, their ability to take care of themselves. No one wants to ever have to deal with this horrible disease, but unfortunately, many of us will get the awful opportunity. There is currently no cure for Alzheimer's, but there are several theories on how to prevent this disease. Some of the newest research is presented in Chapter Ten; Take Good Care of Your Brain.

IATROGENIC DISEASE

Probably the best reason to take responsibility for our health is Iatrogenic Disease, the number three cause of death in the United States, is an inadvertent adverse effect or complication resulting from medical treatment or advice. It can also result from complementary and alternative medicine treatments. How scary is this?

Now please realize that no medical specialist is knowingly putting you at risk, but when you consider that doctors, nurses, physician assistants and practitioners are human and many are overwhelmed with patient loads, it's understandable. Also, many people die of infections they contracted at the hospital while they were receiving treatment. All the more reason for us to take charge of our health and make sure we communicate with our doctors and try as best we can to stay OUT of the hospital unless absolutely necessary. They are there to help us recover from disease or manage chronic conditions and are a part of our team, not the dictators. They are not responsible for our wellness, or to save us from ourselves. That is on us.

As you can see, there are many challenges ahead that might rear their ugly heads as we age. We must remember that we are NOT VICTIMS. We are competing for a quality of life. I have seen many people manage these challenges amazingly well. One thing is for sure, we are not going to live forever so we need to stop acting like it. Don't wait to get a terminal diagnosis to start living life to the fullest. If you were told that you had only one month to live, I'll bet you would do a lot of things in that month and would really begin to appreciate your life and not take it for granted. We can do that now!

CHAPTER THREE

SCOUTING YOUR OPPONENTS:

"No matter what stage of athletic development you are in, you need to get an edge over your competition. If you're working on skill, you want to able to perform the skills of your sport better than your opponent. If you're working on strength, you want to be stronger than the opposition. If you have physical limitations, your edge will come by out-conditioning your opponent."

—Howard Ferguson—The Edge

THEY PLAYED THE GAME LIKE A WELL-OILED MACHINE AND WERE the top club volleyball team in the country. Their coach was a task-master and had honed his skills in Asia, home to the top teams in the world at the time. The athletes were strong, tall, focused, and seemed to all share the same mind when they competed. They had trainers, sponsors, even a team psychologist, and were considered unbeatable. At the end of every club season, there was a high level tournament that featured the top teams in the country—the USVBA Nationals and that year it was in Hawaii. This team was obviously the top seeded team.

Our club team, the Spoilers, had risen to the top ranks after many seasons of struggling, and this year we were stronger than ever, but were no match for the top seeded team. During the season, we played them many times, and only beat them once, which their coach considered a fluke. Little did he know that our coach had a plan that worked in that match that he didn't use again until National Championship Tournament. Every time we played them, he took notes. In fact, we started calling him Mr. Note because he was always writing and we never knew why, until Nationals. You see, he also coached football, and had perfected the fine art of scouting. He knew how to study other teams' strengths, and especially their weaknesses and had studied that team all year. And he saved the best for last.

We made it to the finals in that tournament, and I'll never forget standing on the end line before the start of the match. The other team stood looked like soldiers in formation in their new sweats and stared at us like they were ready to execute us like they had almost every other time that year, but this time, they looked a little more excited—because it was televised and the winner would be the National Champions. We stood there in our shorts and t-shirts from Target, and were just excited just to be there. Before the game began, our coach gave us a new game plan which we noticed was based on his scouting during the year. It seemed too easy to work, but he was our coach, so we trusted him.

His instructions were to serve the line so they couldn't run the middle attack, serve their top hitter short when she was in the front row to take her out of rhythm to spike, to tip short over the middle blocker, and for our strongest hitter to tip deep cross court. He also changed our line up to have different match ups in the frontcourt. I know these instructions don't make very much sense to the non-volleyball player, and they didn't make much sense to us either, but they worked. You see, the opposing team didn't know how to adjust. They just keep doing what they were trained to do and as we executed the game plan, we started getting almost giddy because the unbeatable team started to look scared and panicked.

And we accomplished the impossible—we won the match. Not because we were the better team, but because we had thrown a wrench into their fine-tuned machine. Their coach was so upset that he lost to a bunch of "beach bums" that he threatened to go back to Asia.

So how does this factor into taking on aging as a sport? Getting to know your opposition is imperative if you want to beat them. And the previous chapter listed many conditions and diseases that we will most likely encounter as we age, but what causes them? Like our volleyball opponents—what makes them tick? If we understand the underlying causes of aging, then we can develop a game plan to beat the opposition. Now that's powerful! And remember the goal: To have a high quality of life all the way to the end.

No one wants to take longer to die. What we all want is to live well for as long as we can and feel alive, happy and resourceful. As Sachel Page once said, "How old would you be if you didn't know how old you were?" Wouldn't it be fun to feel like you're thirty, but the calendar says that you're 80? Now that's winning at the game of aging.

THE CAUSES OF AGING

Before we tackle the major causes of aging, know that there are some areas we cannot change, for example, our genes. But we can control genetic expression, and that's exciting. Even though we are stuck with the genes we were given at birth, we can change the way they function. We are dealt a hand at birth, but we get the play the cards, or in some instances, our genes load the gun and lifestyle pulls the trigger. Bruce Lipton's work on *Epigenetics*[1] is very exciting and gives us an incredible sense of empowerment over our health and aging. In his book, acclaimed book, *The Biology of Belief,* he explains the powers of our beliefs and how these may be more important than our genetic make-up.

Also, we can't change our medical history, but we can learn from it, and for most people, when they do get a health scare, they usually wake up and start making different choices to try to prevent these setbacks from happening again. Blaming our genes or wallowing about our past health setbacks will never empower us to live the life we want. However, there is an epidemic of projecting our problems onto other people—like our family members and ancestors. Also, misery loves company, and these blamers and complainers usually hang out together. In sports, we call these people "losers."

Most of the causes of aging are very controllable, if we are willing to make changes in our lifestyle. And the good news is that it is never too late to change your lifestyle for the better. The major causes of aging that are controllable are bad habits, stress, poor nutrition, inflammation, toxins, disuse, radiation, and wear and tear. Address these causes and chances are good that you will see many of the aging symptoms and diseases start to dismantle. It's like throwing a wrench into their machinery, and that's exactly what we want to do.

No one has a perfect lifestyle, and we all have some habits that can accelerate the aging process. However, many of us are searching instead for a quick fix, like a pill, instead of changing a habit. No pill manufactured can ever compensate for a destructive behavior that occurs over and over. I know that it's hard to change, especially if the bad habit has turned into an addiction, but this might be the most powerful change you can make to fight aging. Many of the aging symptoms we complain about are really our poor habits catching up to us. So take a look. What can you change?

My friend, Frank Worm, is part of a group of guys and gals who played volleyball in the 70's and 80's and he has a quote that he says is becoming more important as he gets older as we see many of our friends start to have health issues and pass away as a result of partying too hard, too often, too long. He shared it with me yesterday when he told me that one of our dear friends had passed away from alcohol abuse. His quote is: "You PLAY, YOU PAY." Now Frank wasn't a saint, and did his share of partying, but now he is in total charge of his health and is aging successfully. He goes to the gym, eats healthy, and takes responsibility for his life and health. He was shaking his head when we talked about some of our friends who just kept on partying, drinking and taking recreational drugs, probably because they thought they could do it forever and not suffer any consequences. Not so, especially as we get older.

SMOKING

Probably, one of the most destructive habits is smoking. When we look at the risk factors for all of the major killers, smoking is always on the list. It disrupts every part of your body because nicotine constricts all of the blood vessels, so the cells are not being fed nutrients and oxygen. Nicotine is addictive and has the same relapse rate as heroin. Also, the particulate matter in the cigarettes gets into the lungs, putting people at risk for COPD and cancers of the lungs, throat and mouth.

At least we are starting to see a decrease in smoking for the first time in many years. However, we are seeing an increase in vaping, and that is also scary because of the nicotine.

Why is it so hard for people to stop smoking? The reason is because nicotine causes the brain to release dopamine, which is a feel-good chemical. Where do you think the word dope came from? I know many people who have tried several techniques to quit smoking, and I tell them to keep trying until they find something that works.

When I was growing up it seemed that most adults smoked and many of the shows that were on television had people smoking. Even *The Flintstones*! Fred Flintstone even had an ad: "Winston tastes good like a (snap snap) cigarette should." But I learned when I was 10 years old the horror that cigarettes can inflict and how hard it was to stop.

My Grandma and Grandpop both smoked, and when we would visit them, their house was so full of smoke it looked like thick fog hovering in the rooms. My sweet, fun, Grandpop developed cancer of the larynx and had to have surgery and ultimately was left with a stoma is his throat. I didn't really think much of it until he was back in the hospital because of oral cancer and had another surgery. I remember when I visited him, his mouth was bandaged up, his eyes were swollen and red, and he was smoking through his stoma and the smoke was coming out of his throat. I'll never forget the way he looked at me and I knew that he was scared. It was a picture I will always have in my head. When I asked my dad why Grandpop was still smoking when it was the reason he was sick, he just shook his head with tears in his eyes, and softly said, "...Because he can't stop." After he said that, I decided that I never wanted to go there. Both my grandparents died of smoke-related diseases and it was tragic because it was so preventable. Why didn't we know how dangerous cigarettes were back then?

Also, if you smoke, you probably are finding less and less places to smoke because of the ETS, environmental tobacco smoke. Our college campus is now smoke free, and so are the local beaches and restaurants, even the patios. Why should your habit put someone else at risk? So, if you smoke, make quitting a priority. It will be hard at first, but if you can quit this habit, your life and your health should change dramatically for the better. Also, you might have more friends.

ALCOHOL

Alcohol abuse is another bad habit that can sneak up on us. It's one of those things where a little can be healthy, but a lot can wreck your health and your life. We have heard that a glass of red wine a day can cut our risk of heart disease. But you tell this to a person who loves to drink and they can rationalize drinking a whole bottle of wine, because they really want to protect themselves from heart disease. Unfortunately, it doesn't work that way. Also, as we age, our body doesn't break down alcohol like it used to. The poor liver takes the brunt of alcohol overuse, and eventually can just call it quits.

I'm not saying to never drink. My husband and I love having wine with a special dinner, especially out on the deck with a view of the ocean.

However, we do have to be careful, because it's easy to keep drinking and talking, especially after a hard day teaching. Also, alcohol is immediately absorbed and metabolized, and usually turns to fat and goes to all our storage sites. Fat is easy to store, but hard to burn. Perhaps that's a reason why people struggle to lose weight. Also, we have known for a long time that alcohol kills brain cells. This is scary, because if we live a long life, these brain cells are like gold and we need to protect them.

STRESS

I always ask my students how many of them are stressed out the first week of school and most of them raise their hands. These young people usually have jobs, are going to school, have families and are just spread so thin. Then I ask how many of them have had any stress management education, and no one ever raises his or her hand. I think this is a tragedy. In schools, we are dishing out stress to young people who already have more than they can handle, and we don't give them the tools to manage it. No wonder we have so many problems with drug abuse, depression, homicide, and suicide affecting our youth.

As we get older, stress doesn't go away. It takes on different forms. Instead of worrying about what career we are going to pursue or if we are going to marry and have a family, we are thrown into a new world of uncertainty in terms of how we are going to navigate the challenges of aging. To name a few: When should we retire? What will we do after we retire? Will my pension or 401K be enough to last? What is happening to my body? Why am I having trouble remembering things that used to be easy?

There are two types of stress: one is good stress and the other is bad, or should I say, unhealthy. Acute stress is a survival mechanism and is considered good. If you step out on the curb and a car is coming at you, your body is ready to get out of the way fast. That response is also known as fight or flight and prepares us to battle or run away. All animals have this mechanism and it is used to keep us alive. However, as we know, humans have more problems with stress. Dr. Robert Sapolsky, from Stanford University, the author of *Why Zebras Don't Get Ulcers* has a reason.[2] He says that once the acute stress response is over, like a zebra running for its life with a lion chasing it for food, if the zebra survived, it went back to being normal. It wasn't obsessed about what a jerk the lion was, or spooked about it happening again. It's just OVER! But humans tend to suffer from chronic stress, which is on-going. Most of this stress is in our minds, and it can play havoc with our heath and accelerate aging.

So how can we handle chronic stress? We need to look no further than our own minds, and start doing some housecleaning. Letting go of thoughts and beliefs that no longer serve us is a great start. Also, having a toolbox of stress relievers, such as exercise, meditation, yoga, relaxation methods are also helpful. We'll cover many other stress relievers in the Time Out chapter. For now, just know that chronic stress is one of the fastest ways to age and most of the chronic stresses are self-inflicted. One of my more intelligent friends said that he only feels stress when he doesn't get what he wants, which is quite often.

WEAR AND TEAR

Stuff wears out. Our cars, furniture, house and just about anything else we own. What's cool is if we don't want to repair the damage or restore them back to their original state, we can just dump, trade them in, or sell them and get something new. However, our bodies also suffer from wear and tear, and we can't just trade them in or buy a new one. Darn it! This is the only body we are going to get in this life, so if we want this one to last, we have to be really great at restoring and repairing.

My dad used to buy old cars and restore them as a hobby. I couldn't believe how amazing these old cars looked after he was done with them. They almost looked better than the brand new models and he made a lot of money from this hobby and also was able to have cars for his five children when we were ready to drive. But it took time, work and money to get them back in working condition and make them look like new. However, he was always rewarded with the money he not only made, but saved, and the pride of taking someone's trash and turning it into a treasure.

We can do the same if we just take responsibility for our bodies and don't neglect them. I think a lot of people take better care of their cars than they do their bodies and it shows! Cleaning up our diet, exercise, taking time out to heal, and really listening to our bodies are all good places to start to help with restoration and repairing our bodies. We might not get back to looking like we're 20 again, but we can look a lot better than we do now, and from now on, vow to be the best version of us!

POOR NUTRITION

In the U.S. we have a situation that is taking a toll on everyone, young and old. Most Americans are overweight and malnourished. That doesn't even make any sense, but unfortunately, it's true. How can that be? We don't need to look any further than our food supply, especially, processed foods. Most of these foods are high in calories, sugar and chemicals, and low in nutrients and fiber. As a result, our cells are starving because of the lack of nutrients and our bodies are fatter because we store the extra calories that we don't need.

Back in the 1980's when we noticed the increased rate of heart disease, health officials made a decision to reduce the fat in our diets and ended up with many products that were low fat, no fat, and reduced fat. But since then, our nation is fatter than ever, heart disease is still the number one killer, and now we have a huge problem with diabetes.

So what happened? To compensate for lower fat in foods, we upped the sugar so the food would taste good, and now sugar is in just about every processed food, and that's what most people are eating. Our bodies can't handle all the sugar and chemicals, our cells are starving, and our bodies are getting bigger and bigger. If we want to live a long healthy life, changing our diet is mandatory. We have a whole chapter on nutritional strategies that will hopefully motivate you to fuel your body to survive the challenges of aging. Conscious eating is the key to successful aging, because all body cells need nutrients, and we want to keep them all functioning as best we can as we age.

TOXINS

When it comes to aging and disease, as your cells go, so does your whole body. The two basic causes of cell dysfunction are deficiency of nutrients and toxicity. Think of toxins as garbage building up in your body. While your body is perfectly capable of emptying the trash, it sometimes can't keep up. Is it any wonder when there are over 2,800 additives in processed foods and the Average American takes in about ten pounds a year? And those are just the ones in our food! Toxins are also in polluted air, and many skin and cleaning products. The best thing we can do to eliminate toxins is to not put them into our bodies. Take a look at a food label the next time you are in the store. If you can't pronounce an ingredient or don't know what it is, it's probably an additive, coloring, flavoring, emulsifier, or preservative and your body can only break down a limited amount before it gets overwhelmed. Consider a food label to be a warning label.

INACTIVITY

Also known as "sitting disease", inactivity is another huge age accelerator. With so many Americans having sedentary desk jobs where they are sitting at a computer most of the day, it's no wonder it's a national pastime. And, unfortunately, it is starting younger and younger. I usually ask my college health students how many of them had good physical education programs at their high schools. Out of 45 students, I typically get less than three hands raised. That is so sad, because when we test these students, by doing an easy assessment, a 12 minute run around the track, if they had good cardiovascular fitness, they should be able to complete six laps in twelve minutes. The typical score is 3 1/4 laps, and that is obviously poor and also extremely sad. These students are young! So what's it going to be like when they get older?

When I ask them why they don't exercise, here are the typical reasons: I don't have time, I don't have the money, I don't like it and my favorite: —I don't need it. As we get older, some of the excuses are still there, but the last one doesn't work. Trust me, you need it! One of my favorite things to do at the college is to get students hooked on exercise so it becomes part of their lifestyle. And I'm hoping to do the same in this book. There are so many great resources, workouts and activities that are not only fun, but also incredibly effective in slowing down the aging process and sometimes even reversing it. One thing is for sure—as we take on Aging as a Sport, exercise is not only important, it's no longer optional!

INFLAMMATION

Chronic Inflammation is the new bad kid on the block. It is a major cause of most diseases including the top killers, heart disease, cancer and Alzheimer's. Our bodies are equipped with an immune system, including antibodies and white blood cells and when we are injured or take in a disease causing pathogen, our immune system is stimulated to kill the disease and start the healing process. This is a normal acute response that protects the body from harm and usually has a quick onset and can last anywhere from a few days to a few weeks.

However, chronic inflammation means that the immune system is always turned on, either because whatever was causing the acute inflammation is still present, or there is an irritant of low intensity, or the immune system mistakes normal cells for pathogens causing autoimmune disorders. This can last from several months to years. There are several treatments for chronic inflammation, including taking anti-inflammatory medications although long-term use can cause unwanted side effects. The simplest way to reverse inflammation is through our diet.

Obviously, there are other theories associated with aging, and many of these take a look at specific parts of the cell. One of the most popular theories is that as we age we damage our telomeres, or the end of the chromosomes. Other theories look at specific chemicals or hormones in the body. One excellent website that keeps up on the research on causes of aging, especially at the cellular level is: www.fightaging.com. You can sign up for their newsletter and stay on top of what's going on. I know that I want to know. I'm on the list! You can never know too much when it comes to your life and your health.

Here's a final tip about scouting your opponents. Know what you can control and what you can't. The famous **Prayer of Serenity** says it best:

Grant me the serenity to accept the things I cannot change,

The courage to change the things I can,

And the wisdom to know the difference.

We will focus on changing the things that we can in this book. As you know, we can't control the past or other people, but we can always control ourselves including our lifestyle and attitude. Also, if we are not comfortable with our doctors, we can always get a second opinion or find another doctor. Remember that doctors are human and they don't know everything. One doctor might give you a terminal diagnosis and another doctor will have an answer. My friend, Dan, just got married last year to his college sweetheart, a woman he hadn't seen in over forty years. They have been making up for lost time by acting like frisky teenagers and were incredibly happy, until they found out that he had stage four colon cancer, and his doctor told him at best he had six months to live.

Well, my friend and his wife are fighters, and that diagnosis was over a year ago. He signed up for a new cancer study and also totally changed his diet. He looks better than ever, and even though he is still receiving chemo treatments, the cancer has stopped progressing, and he and his wife make the best of everyday. They are an inspiration as a couple, and are stepping up to the plate to fight this disease, and still acting like frisky teenagers.

CHAPTER FOUR

___

HOLISTIC TRAINING PRINCIPLES

"Success comes from knowing that you did your best to become the best that you are capable of becoming."

—*John Wooden*

E VERYONE AT THE BEACH WAS EXCITED BECAUSE *THEY* WERE COMING! Two of the best female indoor players in the country were going to make their playing debut in the sand at the Hermosa Beach Open Volleyball Tournament. Not only were they Division One Collegiate All- Americans, but were also known worldwide because of their hitting and spiking, and one of the girls was even on the National Team. Tall, athletic and fierce, they were expected to win the tournament easily. However, I wasn't so sure.

The indoor six-man volleyball game is very different from beach doubles. First of all, even though the skills are the same, indoor players tend to specialize. Most of the best hitters indoors can hit straight down at amazing speeds and block high above the net, but many of them are not in the receive serve pattern, which means they don't do much passing. They also do very little setting and they don't have to cover as much court on defense. On the beach, it's the opposite——since there are only two players, these athletes have to be able to do all of the skills, plus have "shots" and be able to play half the court on defense. Also, there are no substitutions in the beach doubles game whereas there are in six person game. If you have to come out of the game, you're done, and so is your team. When you add the environment of heat, sun, wind and the fact that Hermosa sand is among the deepest in the world, I had my doubts that they would do as well as expected if this really was the first time they had competed in the sand.

Watching them play and struggle against beach teams that were almost half their size was both enlightening and entertaining. These premier athletes got their butts kicked, and didn't even make it out of their pool. However, they were good sports and realized that the beach game was a different animal compared to indoors. One of the players never tried beach volleyball again, but the other put in the hard work and eventually had some success.

Even Kerry Walsh, the three-time Olympic Gold Medalist in Beach Volleyball will tell you that for her, transitioning from the indoor game to the beach game was a challenge, but one that she was willing to endure, and now she is one of the best players in the world if not THE BEST!

What does this have to do with aging? Glad you asked. As we transition into this new sport of aging, we need to have more of a holistic approach if we plan to be successful. Just like you need to have all the skills in the beach game, you need to work on all of the dimensions in health, and make some critical changes in your lifestyle if you want be have optimal health as you keep celebrating those birthdays.

As a health professor, I have been teaching dimensions of health and wellness to my students for many years, and it makes perfect sense to have a nice balance of these dimensions as we age. They are the Physical; Mental; Social; Emotional and Spiritual Dimensions of Health and Wellness. Most people think they are healthy as long as they are not sick, but this is only one small part of the picture. Don't you know people who seem to have a healthy, fit body, but they are not happy and certainly don't act healthy? Take Matt for instance: an excellent college student and athlete who received several academic and sports awards. However, he tends to anger easily and finds it hard to communicate with people, even those closest to him. He drinks alcohol heavily, and can't seem to stay in a relationship for any length of time. People like Matt have only one or two of the dimensions working for them and are lacking the others, creating an imbalance in their lives. Can you see the similarity with the world-class indoor volleyball player who could only hit and block but not pass or set on the beach? We have to realize that our lives are not specialized, and we need to be well-rounded if we want to have the best possible life, right up to the end.

THE PHYSICAL DIMENSION OF HEALTH AND WELLNESS

Many people feel that this is the one and only dimension of health and wellness. However, we often just focus and obsess about how we look on the outside. I wonder if that would change if we had a mirror that reflected back not only how we looked on the outside but on the inside too. Doctors routinely test our blood, our heart, blood pressure, lung capacity, and urine, to find out how our body is functioning. Also, our bodies send messages to us all the time and often talked to us when we were competing in our sport and we usually listened. As a result we fine-tuned our training to address what was going on inside because it affected our performance. Our nutrient intake, physical activities, and sleep all affect our physical health and performance so now especially, we need to tune in again, and make sure we are giving the body what it needs to perform everyday tasks.

THE MENTAL DIMENSION OF HEALTH AND WELLNESS

We have all heard of the mind-body connection, but still people tend to focus only on the body and let the mind run amok. What if your cells were listening to your thoughts? Do you think your cells would be happy and healthy? The answer is "NO" if your thoughts are constantly negative. Well guess what? You cells DO listen to your thoughts, so doing some housecleaning is imperative as we age.

I remember hearing about a study when I was a student at UCLA that showed just how much the mind can influence the body. There was a man who had just been given a terminal diagnosis, stage four cancer and his doctor told him that there was nothing he could do so he should put his affairs in order. However, this man was determined to live and fight, and coincidentally, there was a double blind research study being held at a neighboring hospital that was asking for volunteers to test a new cancer- fighting drug.

He called and tried to join the study, but they rejected him because his cancer was too advanced. But he kept calling, every day in fact, and begged to get into the study saying that he would be their best patient and do whatever they asked. Finally, they relented, but if you know anything about these kind of studies, then you know that there are two groups, one is the experimental group that is actually taking the drug they are testing, and the other group is the control group, where the participants think they are taking the drug, but they are taking something that looks like the drug. No one knows which group they are in except for the people doing the study.

Well, it's not hard to guess which group he was assigned to—the control group. But remember, *he thought* he was taking the drug and was so excited and motivated to beat the cancer that he went into remission! The organizers of the study were shocked and confused—why was his cancer gone? He wasn't even taking the drug! But it wasn't the drug--- it was his belief in the drug that cured him of his cancer. Isn't that cool?

Our minds are much more powerful than we realize, and that is why it is so important to train our minds the same way we train our bodies. Expecting positive outcomes is a huge part of living a healthy, optimal life, especially as we age. However, we often see the reverse as people start to get up in years. My own daughter was complaining when she turned 35 that she felt so "old" and was depressed on her birthday. OMG! I had a long talk with her——"You are beautiful, vibrant, have an amazing husband, a great job, a beautiful home and an amazing son. Your age is not stamped on your forehead, besides, who the heck said that 35 was old?" I think I snapped her out of it—seriously? 35?

If we think we are old, we will start to act like it, and the body will follow. Don't go that route! I don't care what the calendar says and neither should you.

And also, realize that we still need to keep learning as we age. I get amused when I hear some of my colleagues say that they don't need to learn technology skills, and are just fine with teaching "old school." Nothing wrong with old school, however, if we don't keep up with technology, we will get run over by the next generation. Trust me, the kids these days have grown up with technology and are great at it. This comes in handy when my computer, doc cam, and projector don't work— which happens rather often. Instead of calling our ITT department, I'll ask my students if anyone knows how to fix the problem. It's a little embarrassing sometimes when it's a simple adjustment, like clicking on an icon, but I don't mind asking for help since I always have several students who volunteer their services. Even though they are the masters of tech and I'm not, at least I'm using it with my teaching and am getting better every day. Who knows, I might eventually even catch up to my students.

Setting goals, planning, learning, reframing our stressors, focusing, clearing our mind of clutter are all important skills we need. The mind will stay active if we exercise it, just like our bodies. We'll talk more about brain health and how to keep the brain active in Chapter 10, Take Good Care of Your Brain.

THE SOCIAL DIMENSION OF HEALTH AND WELLNESS

Healthy relationships and communication skills are much more important to our overall health than we think. Getting along with others, accepting differences and other points of view, and being a good listener are essential to our health and happiness. As we age, we need to make sure we surround ourselves with people who are positive and supportive of our goals. No one wants to hang around people who complain all the time, so we might need to seek out some new friends.

When you played your sport, you were most likely on one or several teams, and probably developed close friendships as a result. When you go through the tough times of competition experiencing the highs of winning and the lows of losing, it's nice to have people who support you and have your back.

But as we go on to our careers, those close friendships often dissipate because our lives change so much and we often lose touch. In fact, one of the most common complaints that older people mention is that they are lonely and depressed. What we need is to join a new team, with people who have the same goals. The chapter on Team Building is fun, and there are many ways to find people who are just like you, and who want to enjoy life to the fullest and not let age get in the way.

THE EMOTIONAL DIMENSION OF HEALTH AND WELLNESS

This is the feeling component, and refers to the ability to deal constructively with your feelings and the feelings of others. It also includes knowing how to cope with problems that arise in life, and how to endure and manage stress. This is the one dimension that is often a struggle and one for which people usually don't ask for help or know how to manage. Emotional states can set the stage for disease by lowering the body's resistance. The amazing thing is that how we choose to feel is well within our control because we don't feel an emotion until we attach a meaning

Chapter Four - Holistic Training Principles

to the stressor. Any stressor that is not life threatening is one that we can choose to either get upset about and do something about it, or let it go.

THE SPIRITUAL DIMENSION OF HEALTH AND WELLNESS

This dimension refers to the ability to balance your inner needs with the demands of the rest of the world. It is directly related to the ability to understand and express one's purpose in life. To appreciate life and learn from its experiences, to have unity with the environment, to develop a sense of internal values and to trust in the universe or a supreme being are all a part of this important component. Many people think that you have to have a religion in order to experience spirituality but that is not necessarily the case. I know a lot of people who are not religious, but have incredible spirituality and some who are very religious and have zero spirituality. So realize that you can have both, neither, or one or the other. They are not mutually exclusive.

I remember reading this enlightening piece of advice in several of Dr. Wayne Dyer's books: *Instead of thinking that you are a human being having a spiritual experience, consider that you might be a spiritual being having a human experience.* When I share that quote with my students some of them get really excited. We can do this!

Here are more principles that most athletes, coaches and business people all adhere to that guide them to success. They are certainly relevant as we age. Most of us are familiar with them and have used them in the past. We just need to reactivate them with our new challenges ahead.

MODERATION

Does anyone teach moderation anymore? It certainly doesn't appear that way. It seems that we either do way too much or way too little in most endeavors. A perfect example is our food intake——we are either

59

taking in way too much, too often, or are on a restrictive diet and eat hardly anything. We even have a new eating disorder, Orthorexia, where these people are so overly concerned about what's in their food, that they become obsessed with eating only "perfect food" and as a result don't take in enough calories to be healthy.

If you were an athlete chances are good that you learned to listen to your body and knew when you were overtraining or doing too much. Obviously, that is a sign to take a break. You also knew the foods that fueled your performance and the ones that made it tougher to compete. You also knew when you weren't doing enough to improve your game, and were getting lethargic with training. Somewhere in the middle is usually best. Just like Goldilocks—"this one is too hot, this one is too cold, and this one is just right!" Moderation—it is a simple but underused principle that is golden.

MOTIVATION

As an athlete, I have experienced a lot of coaches utilizing different methods to motivate me while I was on their team. Some used fear, and at times it was effective, especially when it wasn't used often. It usually shocked us back into focusing, however I had one coach who used it all the time, and after a while, we tuned her out. Although she was entertaining, especially when she pulled her hair and screamed when we made an error it was ineffective. I remember one junior coach who told her kids that whenever they made a mistake, the whole team had to do push-ups before the next play. I felt so bad for these kids during our match against them because they were so sore from doing all the push-ups that they couldn't even serve the ball over the net.

What usually works best is to focus on what we want, instead of what we don't want. Obviously if we get a diagnosis of a medical condition or disease, then yes, that fear of succumbing to it can step us up into high gear and suddenly make us take responsibility. That's a healthy fear. What isn't healthy is worrying all the time about —what if this happens? If it hasn't happened yet, then focus on the quality of life that you want now. Do you want to travel? Play with your grandkids? Learn a new skill? Have lots of energy? Feel great in your body? Knock down that bucket list? Take up a new hobby? Mentor? Spend more quality time with your loved ones? Volunteer your services? There's a lot to go for so don't ruin it by using fear. Most of the things we fear will happen never do, so instead, focus on the target——optimal living until the end!

BIO-INDIVIDUALITY

In 1970, Roger Williams published *Biochemical Individuality,* a book that introduced a concept called bio-individuality. He proposed that individuality permeates each part of the human body and that we have personal differences in anatomy, metabolism, composition of bodily fluids and cell structure. He concluded that as a result, each person has genetically determined and highly individualistic nutrition requirements.[1]

Guess what? This theory has been largely ignored by mainstream medicine and completely ignored by food manufacturers. Why was it ignored? The reason is because it was not profitable, especially for the food manufacturers. They want their foods to be for everyone! However, even though we are the same in many ways, we also have many differences, and that can explain why one person's food is another person's poison (peanuts anyone?) and why some fitness programs work for some and not others (fast twitch vs. slow twitch muscle fiber ratios) and why some medications work for some patients and not others. Keeping this in mind, it becomes our journey to find the best options that work for us personally.

PERSISTENCE

My husband's mantra is "persistence equals success." He teaches this to his students and athletes and was incredibly persistent in being patient when it came to our relationship. He is eight years older than me, and wanted to marry me before I was even interested in him. In fact, he asked proposed twice and I said no, both times, but we still dated. He could have easily given up but he didn't. I finally came out of my fog, and realized what an amazing person he was, and we have been married now for forty years.

I have always told my students and athletes to never give up on anything until you reach your goal or get something better. The reason persistence is so important in the aging game, is because it is never over until the end. We just keep playing the game, and give it our best effort each and every day. Vince Lombardi, the famous football coach has another great quote: "If you persist and give your all, you'll never lose, but sometimes the clock will run out."

SPECIFICITY

Going after what you want and having a plan is important for any goal and all athletic coaches have game plans against each team their athletes will face. Whatever health challenge is ahead of us is going to require a specific plan to beat it. Prevention is always a huge key, but if we are diagnosed with a serious disease or condition, we need to buckle down, get focused and do what it takes to keep our health and quality of life.

BE GRATEFUL FOR WHAT YOU HAVE

I can't emphasize this enough. The Attitude of Gratitude is one of the most important qualities we can have in our lives. Unfortunately, we are surrounded with people and media influences that make us feel bad for not having more.

We don't have to look any further than the people who both tolerate and love us. We should show some appreciation for having them in our lives instead of taking them for granted. Also, appreciate our amazing bodies and how they have tolerated our unhealthy lifestyles for so long, and are just waiting for us to finally take care of them.

I have my yoga students keep a journal during the semester, and they can only write positive things in it—no venting. At first it's hard for them because they are so used to looking for what's wrong, but after a couple of weeks, they start looking for positive things in their lives.

Don't you hate being around complainers? It's like a dark cloud is following them around raining slime on them. I know I do, and there are a lot of older people who spend a lot of time complaining about their lives. They love sharing misery, and if you spend too much time with them, you'll feel like they are sucking the energy right out of you. Actually, they are—-I call them energy vampires.

I found a technique that works well with these people. Instead of asking "How are you?" Instead ask: "What's new and good?" It actually stops them from dumping their psychic trash on you and may also help them to stop complaining. I have a little saying from the ancient Greeks that I share with my yoga students: "Look for the good and you will find it; Look for the bad and you will find that too." It's our choice.

CAUSE AND EFFECT

I'm sure you've heard of Karma, in fact, I would like to have that job. Don't you get upset when the good people get screwed and the obnoxious, horrible people seem to have everything handed to them? I sometimes fantasize about being the entity that gets to dish out the consequences and rewards. If the job ever opens up, I will be the first in line to apply.

However, after being here for many years, I realize it takes time for the cause and effect catch up. We just have to be patient and realize that effort and hard work is always eventually rewarded. We just can't attach ourselves to knowing exactly how it's going to play out. So be patient, and don't worry about how unfair life seems at times. We all get our rewards and consequences for our choices... often not at the same time, and often not when we want or expect them.

SELF-DISCIPLINE

I can't believe how many people put their lives and health into the hands of others, most notably, their doctors. Trust me, doctors can only do so much and cannot compensate for our poor life-style choices. Their job is to save lives, not move us to optimal health. *That's our job.*

Some of us have gotten along without having much self-discipline, especially if we are conditioned to being told what to do by others. We have to develop self-discipline as we age. I know some people who are taking life-saving medications, like insulin, and are totally irresponsible with their eating habits and keeping their blood sugars within a healthy range——they are taking chances with their lives but for some reason think that the doctor will fix them on their next visit. Remember, this is YOUR life, not theirs. They have many other patients beside you.

NO EXCUSES

Along with putting too much responsibility into our doctor's hands, we also usually have a whole list of excuses that we have used in our lives to keep the pressure off. "It's my parent's fault, I can't afford to eat healthy, exercise hurts, no one cares, I'm too old to have any energy." As athletes we might have rationalized a loss by placing blame on the officials, the coach, or another teammate, but eventually we realized that it did not make us better at our game. So we learned the hard way that excuses don't produce winners. Many of us have rationalized and projected our problems and faults onto others for so many years so we that we don't even realize what we are doing. The bottom line is that we are accountable. Just remember that if you want to change your life for the better, making excuses for your state of health doesn't give you any power. As we age, we can no longer put off the consequences of our choices. We have to stop making excuses, and start looking at what got us to where we are today and how we are going to change for the better.

I had a student a while back named Donna. She was in her mid-fifties, but you'd never know it. She was a vibrant woman with the cutest smile and the biggest laugh in the world. She came back to school to learn, get in shape and pursue new interests. Her personality attracted many students and she soon had more friends than she knew what to do with. She was also a very large woman and said that all the women in her family were heavy. One of her goals was to have a "normal-sized" casket when she died, since all of her relatives needed the super-size.

I thought she was kidding but then I found out that she had an inoperable brain condition and her time was limited. She was a student in three of my fitness classes and worked out harder than most of my younger pupils. Several times I had to tell her to slow down because I was afraid that she was going to drop dead in my class. But she just gave me that huge smile and kept on working out, perhaps a little slower. Donna became an icon at school, appearing to get younger every day. She changed her hair, lost weight, and finally graduated with her degree. We were all amazed and delighted with her success. One day, I received news that Donna's aneurysm ruptured and that she had passed away in her sleep. She'd gone to bed one night and didn't wake up, but I'm sure she did awake in heaven. If there was ever a person that did not let age or infirmities stand in her way, it was this wonderful woman. She showed everyone who knew her how to have an ageless life. And yes, she got a normal-sized casket.

OFFENSE VERSUS DEFENSE

The coach was known as an offensive genius. His Run and Gun shooting style offense was designed to score over 100 points in each and every game. When he was hired for our local NBA team, people were excited about seeing a fast, offensive, Showtime style game. He delivered on his run and gun style and most of the time when the team got the ball, they shot it within eight seconds. But unfortunately, the players missed a lot of shots, didn't rebound and couldn't get down to the other side of the court to stop the opponents from doing easy layups. The scores were high, and many of the opponents had season high scores when they played against our team. After a while, it became apparent to everyone that one very important factor was missing—it was defense. No wonder the other teams were able to win so easily. They didn't have anyone stopping them from getting to the basket.

Every athlete who plays a sport usually prefers to play offense over defense. After all, making a basket, getting a kill in volleyball, a goal in soccer, a touchdown in football is how the team scores and the highest score wins. However, when teams are close in ability, athleticism and desire, it is usually defense that wins. Preventing the other team from scoring is a huge part of playing a game, and one that usually does not get the attention it deserves.

In the aging game, we must be proficient at both offense and defense. Offense is important to keep us in charge of our lives and empower us to be the healthiest we can be. It's the pro-active approach. Defense is keeping the opponents from either killing us or taking away our quality of life. We usually don't want to be reactive, but if one of these monsters is our opponent, we need a great defensive plan along with our offense.

So how do we play defense? First of all, we need to understand our opponent. If you were scouting an athletic team, you would know their tendencies, strengths, and weaknesses. You would need to have a special plan, just for this team. While one offense might be effective against one opponent, it won't work against every opponent. That's why you need to know everything you can about whatever challenge you are facing, and make sure you have people who will help you design the best defensive plan. A great example is cancer. A cancer diagnosis is scary, and there are many ways to fight and defeat this opponent. Obviously, you will need to have a great medical support team that is familiar with the type of cancer that was diagnosed, and has had success at treating it. The amazing thing about cancer is that there are so many new treatments that we did not have a decade ago. So, getting a second or third opinion is not only advised, but also sometimes necessary to develop the best plan.

Remember that knowledge is power, but not useful unless we act on it. Understanding our opponents and their weaknesses and strengths is not enough---we have to take action.

CHAPTER FIVE

EXERCISE IS NO LONGER OPTIONAL

"Life is a game of survival of the fittest; the strong will survive. It's not how much talent you have, but how much of it you make use of and what kind of physical condition you are in."

—*Mike Pruitt*

WHAT IF I TOLD YOU THAT I HAD A PILL THAT COULD RELIEVE STRESS and depression, help you lose weight, regenerate brain cells, prevent heart disease, type two diabetes and certain cancers, boost confidence, give you more energy, reverse most of the symptoms of aging and it had no side effects. Would you take it? Most of my students say: "Yes of course!"...That is until they hear the directions. "Every day, take one pill with an 8 ounce glass of water 15 minutes before exercising for at least a half hour." Then they start shaking their head with a knowing smile on their faces.

As you have probably guessed, it's not what's in the pill, it's the directions: take before *exercising for 30 minutes every day.* Would it work? Yes! But some of the benefits are going to take time to see. The problem with most people is that they want instant results, and anyone who can guarantee this is usually going to get their attention and money. What works instead is to have exercise as a daily activity, just like brushing your teeth. We wouldn't go for days without brushing our teeth because our mouth would become offensive to others and probably start to hurt after a few days.

Instead of adhering to a lifestyle exercise program, too many people confine their exercise to: jumping to conclusions, running up bills, stretching the truth, lying down on the job, sidestepping responsibility and pushing their luck. Some of my students say that they used to exercise a lot when they were on athletic teams, but don't have the time to do it anymore because of their studies and work. And I usually ask, "How's that working for you? Are you tired, stressed out? Gaining weight? Feeling depressed?" As they keep nodding to all my questions it starts to sink in that they can't store fitness and maybe they should start working out again. It really doesn't take much to see results...just a commitment to doing it every day. So, exercise needs to be a part of our lifestyle, and we need to make it fun, not something we dread.

My students who do exercise say that the most important reason is because it makes them feel GREAT! What an awesome reason to work out.

In the last chapter we talked about the dimensions of health and wellness and how you needed to have a balance of all the dimensions in order to have optimal health. The same goes with exercise and fitness. In order to be truly fit, and get all the benefits, (and as an athlete, why would you want any less?)—you must have all the components of fitness—Cardiorespiratory Endurance, Muscle Fitness including Muscle Strength and Endurance, Flexibility, and Body Composition.

The cool thing these days is that you can work all of the fitness components in one workout. There are also several activities that are challenging, innovative and fun! Remember that we are all different in what works for us and what we will enjoy doing. One of my students didn't like any fitness activities and then I reminded her that she could get great results from something as fun as dancing. She said that she used to love to dance, but didn't have time anymore. When we checked her schedule, we found that she had the time available to take one of our popular fitness classes, Country Western Aerobics. She signed up and met new people, lost weight and felt great! Now she is an instructor and gets to do it every day!

CARDIORESPIRATORY ENDURANCE

This is the most important of all the fitness components because it is systemic, meaning that it affects all the systems in the body. Simply put, CR Endurance is the ability of the heart and lungs to transport oxygen and food to the cells and eliminate waste products so the cells can live and do their jobs. Sounds easy, huh?

However, the heart and the lungs are the organs that are most negatively affected by a poor lifestyle as evidenced by the high number of heart attacks and chronic lung disease. How can we strengthen our Cardiorespiratory Endurance? By performing prolonged, large muscle dynamic exercise at moderate to high levels of intensity. There are many ways to improve Cardiorespiratory Endurance, and we are all different in what works for us and what is safe.

What are some of the benefits of having good Cardiorespiratory Fitness? These are just a few:

Lower risk of heart disease

Reduced risk of diabetes

Lower blood pressure

Lower risk of certain cancers

Increased bone density

Increased energy

Psychological benefits including reducing depression and anxiety

Assists in weight control

When people train to get Cardiorespiratory Endurance, they often do exercises such as jogging and playing sports. This is usually fine for people who enjoy these activities, however, as we get older, we need to be aware of activities that can cause injury and overuse problems for the weight bearing joints, especially the knees and the hips.

I used to love to jog, play indoor volleyball, teach high impact aerobics and did these activities for many years. However, I can't do these activities anymore because of my knees. I wore out my cartilage and now have arthritis in both knees and it's downright painful if I try any of these activities. However, that doesn't stop me from working out. I just shifted into activities that didn't cause as much impact on my joints. I do my jogging in the soft sand, use a Curve machine at the gym that has no impact and can work the leg muscles like you wouldn't believe, do a lot of rowing, and also biking. I love to mix things up so I don't get bored and often go from one exercise to another. I want to have good fitness, especially for my heart and lungs, but don't want to injure myself doing activities that my body doesn't respond to anymore.

Other activities include swimming, skiing, skating, walking, boxing and even walking. Moving our bodies is what they were made to do. We just need to make sure we don't do too much and cause injury:

HERE ARE SOME SIGNS OF A GOOD WORKOUT:

Breathing is controlled and comfortable

You feel like you can work at the same pace for an extended time

Shortly after the workout, you feel revitalized and full of energy

You have a good night's sleep after the workout and wake up refreshed

Any muscle soreness disappears when moving

HERE ARE SOME SIGNALS OF OVEREXERTION:

Severe breathlessness

Undue fatigue during exercise

Dizziness, nausea or feeling faint

Severe muscle soreness

Pain or tightness in the chest or extremely fast or irregular heartbeats (these require a doctor's immediate attention)

Inability to sleep at night and wake up the next morning feeling fatigued

Elevated resting heart rate

You are extremely hungry, even if you have had regular meals

Extreme fatigue for the rest of the day following the workout

If you are starting an exercise program, remember to start slowly. I see a lot of students sign up for an activity class, and end up doing too much too soon; especially former athletes who are accustomed to working out hard but haven't done so for a long time. You can always do more if you want as your body starts to adapt.

One activity that most of us can do in our everyday life is walking and is especially important for those who spend a lot of time sitting during the day. A current guideline is for us to get at least 10,000 steps a day. This really isn't that hard to do, and it is easy to track with a pedometer. There are lots of apps on our cell phones that will track our steps and even chart them for weeks and months. Walking is so simple that people found it hard to believe that it is a great way to get fitness benefits, especially for beginners. Some of the benefits of walking include:

1. There is no new skill to master.

2. It can be done anywhere.

3. Walking does not require any equipment, other than shoes.

4. Most of the body's large muscles are involved.

5. There is no risk of injury, unless you don't look where you are going or are in an unsafe area.

6. Walking enhances creativity and reduces stress.

7. It can be done alone or with others.

8. Walking burns between 300 and 400 calories an hour.

9. Walking strengthens bones and may prevent osteoporosis.

10. It's a great activity for the overweight individual, since it burns calories and is easy to do.

11. Walking can double as a moving meditation.

The bottom line is that in order to strengthen our heart and lungs to be able to move nutrients and oxygen to our cells, we need to move our muscles—the more the better.

MUSCLE STRENGTH AND ENDURANCE

"Use it or Lose it." We have all heard this phrase, and it applies directly to muscle mass and aging. As we age, if we do not exercise, we lose between 1/4 and 1/2 pound of muscle a year. Muscle mass tends to peak in the early twenties and declines after age forty. This muscle loss is one reason why people become frail as they get older and tend to also get fatter. By the age of 65, muscle mass and strength declines by about 20% if a person does not exercise.

People think we get fat and frail because of age, but the truth is, that we age because we get fat and frail. What's great about resistance training is that you are never too old to get results. We can reverse this decline and even build new muscle, no matter how old we are.

No fitness program is complete without resistance training. What is really cool about lifting weights is that all of the major muscles in the body can be exercised in just 15 - 20 minutes. Twice a week is enough to see results from an effective balanced weight training program.

So what results are we talking about?

1. Increases basal metabolic rate....in other words causes the body to burn more calories at rest.

2. Improves self- image.

3. Decreases the risk of osteoporosis.

4. Offsets muscle imbalances.

5. Prevents the loss of muscle mass that occurs with aging.

6. Encourages people to go to failure. (Failure in weight training means doing a particular exercise until you can no longer lift with good form.) Failure is associated with success.

7. Resistance exercises burn calories during the workout and after the workout is over.

8. Everyday activities become easier.

9. Heightens kinesthetic awareness and sensitivity to our body's needs. You will definitely be able to feel muscles you never thought you had before.

10. Weight training provides shapely, firm muscles that cannot be obtained by dieting or aerobic exercise alone.

11. Because women have low levels of the male hormone testosterone, they DO NOT get excessively large muscles from weight training. The muscles respond by increasing in density instead. Women tend to lose inches, slim down and get a more defined body. If women only do aerobic training, they will go from being a large pear to a smaller pear, but not change the shape of the body.

Muscle strength and muscle endurance are two characteristics of muscle fitness. Muscle strength refers to the amount of force a muscle can overcome and muscle endurance is how long a muscle can contract without tiring or hold a sustained contraction. There is an obvious overlap in these characteristics because if a person decides to train for strength, muscle endurance and tone will also improve, and if a person decides to train for endurance and tone, some improvement may also occur in muscle strength. The cool thing is that you can work these two characteristics separately or both at the same time. The usual prescriptions for working muscle strength is to lift heavy weights (85-100% of a repetition max) using a low number of reps, and for muscle endurance, to use lighter resistance and more repetitions. To get a balance of both, lift a moderate amount of weight that you can manage for between 8 and 12 repetitions.

In order to have a well-rounded resistance training program, all of the muscle groups must be challenged, not just the visible or easy ones. I have seen people at the gym just work the biceps and ignore the triceps, the chest and not the upper back, and the quadriceps and not the hamstrings. Remember that muscles work in pairs and must be balanced in order to prevent injury. If one part of the pair is significantly stronger than the other, postural problems, injury and joint dislocations could occur.

The basic muscle group pairs are: abdominals/erector spinae (lower back), quadriceps/hamstrings, biceps/triceps, pectorals/ trapezius and rhomboids, abductors (outer thigh)/ adductors (inner thigh) and deltoid/lats. You don't have to remember the muscle names to have a balanced program. Just make sure if you do a push exercise, that you counterbalance it with a pull exercise, in other words, if you do a shoulder press, make sure you do a lat pull down, if you do a bench press, do a row.

Picture your body as though it were a blob of clay. Now, with the imagination of a sculptor, design the shape of a body that you desire. Do you want a fuller, more defined upper body and a smaller waist and hip measurement, larger calves, smaller, more toned thighs? Muscle sculpting is an art, and with resistance training, once you understand a few easy principles, you can shape your body anyway you want. Just remember that because of bio-individuality, different programs work for different people, and the time it takes to see results and the extent of the changes possible also vary. However, the good news is that we can all improve, and it doesn't matter how old we are to see results.

My husband, Pat, is called Mega Man at the gym. He is 74 years old, has a full head of white hair in a Beatles hair style, is medium height, has a little belly, but can lift more weight than men half his age. It's amusing to watch him go to a weight machine and do his reps, especially after a young male Adonis just finished. People just stop and watch as my husband adds more weight and does his set. They can't believe their eyes!

But he wasn't always like this. You see, about 15 years ago he had gained a bunch of weight when we were both teaching all day and then coaching in the evenings and on the weekends. He was a former athlete and was frustrated with his body and wanted to do something about it. So I got him a membership to the local gym for Christmas and said that he had to find some time to use it, or I wouldn't renew it. Well, he's been going almost every day since then, and has lost over forty pounds and has made a commitment to not lose muscle mass as he ages. He even has goals as to how much he wants to lift in each muscle group by the time he is seventy five. When he comes home from the gym, if it was a good day meeting his goals, he wears a shirt that says "BEAST" and smiles. I don't have to ask how he did. So, it's never too late to start to improve muscle mass.

When people ask me what weight training program they should try, I always tell them to start with a combination program that works both strength and endurance. As people progress, they can do more reps and sets and add more resistance as they adapt. Then, they ask what resistance program I do for myself, and to tell you the truth, I am all over the place because I love variety, and get bored easily. However, I tried a new resistance workout recently and am blown away by how effective it is, how little time it takes and the fact that it is very safe for anyone to do.

My dad shared a book with me and told me to check it out: It's called *The Slow Burn Fitness Revolution*. Well, the word "revolution" caught my eye and but the sub title almost ruined it for me——"The Slow Motion Fitness Revolution That Will Change Your Body in 30 Minutes a Week."[1]

I immediately thought to myself (You must be kidding---only 30 minutes a week?) If it sounds too good to be true, it probably is, but I still wanted to try it since my Dad is 91 years old and looks and acts 30 years younger. So I read the book and decided to give it a try. Why not? I've tried just about everything else.

The program involves resistance training that you can do either at home or at the gym. I decided to do it at the gym since that's where I have my favorite machines and routine. I normally do either high endurance straight sets—at least 15 reps a set, or pyramids, which involve changing the weight on each set-- high reps on low weight and low reps on high weight.

But this is totally different! You only need to do three repetitions for each exercise, but you do them *really, really, really* slow. They recommend you do the exercise with a metronome so you keep the slow pace, but I decided just to count. So my first exercise was my usual favorite, the lat pulldown machine. I found the weight--- that I should be able to work with for 90 seconds. It was 70 pounds and I was ready to begin. The gym was rather full at the time, and I was a regular, but I felt a little uneasy trying something so out of the ordinary for me.

I took a long breath and then started my first slow burn set-----down for an inch, hold for three seconds, and then lower all the way one inch at a time for seven seconds, and then without stopping, raise it another inch for three seconds, and then go all the way back up for a slow count of seven seconds........I did the three sets, but it was one of the hardest things I have ever done with weights! My muscles had a burning feeling I had never experienced before. I guess that was the "slow burn."

According to the book, the authors want you to go to fatigue or failure, which I am used to, but there I was---after three reps, in total failure! I couldn't believe it! But I was excited! I went and did the rest of my normal exercises using the slow burn, and it was hilarious because all the other people who were doing their lifts were going so fast in comparison.

By the end of my workout, 30 minutes, my body felt incredible---challenged but also regenerated. I felt taller and stronger even two days after the workout.

So if you are ready to try something different in your resistance training or are just getting started, I encourage you to try the SLOW BURN. It really is revolutionary!

Make sure that whatever resistance-training program you choose, that you know how to do the exercises and lifts properly. If you are unsure about any piece of equipment, ask for help. It's a good investment to hire a trainer, especially when starting a program. Here are a few safety guidelines that most experts recommend.

1. Breathe properly, Exhale on exertion and inhale during relaxation. Never hold your breath while training with weights.

2. Move only the parts of the body that are supposed to be moving in an exercise. No cheating!

3. Use the full range of motion on all lifts.

4. Warm the muscles up before you lift.

5. A muscle requires at least two days of rest to recover and adapt before it should be exercised again. Do not work a muscle group more than three times a week or every other day.

6. Exercise the larger muscles first and the smaller muscles last. The larger muscles need the smaller ones to assist the movement so you don't want them to fatigue first.

7. Listen to your body. If you become very sore or experience severe or chronic pain, this is NOT normal or desirable.

8. Never sacrifice form to add more weight.

9. When picking up a weight from the ground, keep your back straight and your head up. Lift with your legs.

10. Make sure your diet is fueling your workout. You can't build muscles out of sugar.

11. The most common cause of injury in resistance training is over-training, so make sure you don't do too much too soon or overwork the muscles, especially when they are already fatigued.

12. If you are new to the gym, get a good trainer, especially if you have any limitations. Make sure your trainer offers modifications and writes a program just for you.

The following is a sample workout for an unconditioned person who is new to resistance training. One exercise for each major muscle group is recommended for beginners. Choose a weight that can be lifted in a range of 8 - 12 reps. Once you can easily lift the weight 12 times or more, it's time to add more resistance.

Bench Press

Shoulder Press

Seated Row

Lat Pull down

Bicep Curl

Triceps Extension

Leg Press

Calf Press

Abdominal Curls

Low Back Press

Obviously, there are advanced systems since weight training has become both an art and a science. Some of the more advanced systems are: The Double Progressive System, Circuit Weight Training, HIIT with Resistance, Super Sets, Giants, Pyramid Training, Muscle Confusion, Forced Reps, and Twenty Ones. These are just some of the programs and methods out there, and more are being developed all the time. The bottom line is to find a resistance program that you like, is safe, and gives you results.

FLEXIBILITY

This is imperative to work on as we age, because our movement capabilities depend not only on muscle functioning, but the range of motion present at our joints. As we get up in years, if we don't work on flexibility, we will find it hard to move to do the simplest tasks, like getting up off the floor. Flexibility is just as important as cardiovascular endurance, and muscle strength and endurance. What's cool is that flexibility can be a part of any other workout or sport in which you participate since people normally do stretching exercises before and also sometimes after the activity.

Flexibility varies from person to person, and from joint to joint in the same person. That is normal. What we want is to improve or keep what we have, not try to be more flexible than others. Having good range of motion in the joints not only decreases the risk of injury, it is also a great way to reduce stress.

To improve flexibility, there are many types of stretching techniques. Static stretching is slowly stretching a muscle and holding the stretched position. Dynamic stretching is moving the joints slowly through their range of motion in a controlled manner. Proprioceptive neuromuscular facilitation involves contracting a muscle before it is stretched to obtain a greater range of motion. There are many activities that are fun and can improve flexibility tremendously. Just make sure the intensity is pain -free. *No pain, no gain* is not a training principle for improving flexibility. In fact, it's a sure fire way to get injured because if we overstretch our ligaments that hold the joints together, they are not going back to where they were before. How many dancers and gymnasts do you know who overstretched their body when they were young only to now have joint problems because of the instability caused by over-stretching?

Here are some tips for stretching:

1. When doing a static stretch, hold the stretch, relax and breathe.

2. Remember to never stretch to the point of pain.

3. Keep the back in a neutral position (keep its' natural curve).

4. When possible, contract the muscle opposite the one being stretched. This may enhance the relaxation of the muscle that is being stretched.

5. Do not compare yourself to others. Be content to work within your limits.

6. Balance your stretches just like you would balance your resistance exercises.

7. Stretching is most effective if you do it every day.

8. Exhale when going into the stretch to facilitate relaxation.

9. If possible, close your eyes and tune into the muscle being stretched.

10. Never bounce when stretching. That could cause injury.

There are no other restrictions and we can stretch every day—in fact, that is the best prescription. However, it's always best to warm up the muscle before stretching—think of your tendons and muscles as "taffy." You wouldn't want to pull taffy if it was cold——SNAP!

After teaching yoga for over 15 years, I have seen incredible improvements in flexibility in my students, especially in the area of lower back. If fact, this is the most reported benefit consistently listed. Lower back problems plague our society because most activities don't stretch and work the spine. As a result, instead of working on flexibility, too many people turn to pain relievers to rectify the problem. Yoga is one of the few activities that moves and stretches the spine in every range of motion. I have seen many students no longer take medications for their back pain as a result of a consistent yoga practice.

One of my trainers once said: "You are only as old as your spine." I thought that was a bit strange, but as I see a lot of people struggle with pain and movement problems because of back problems, I'm starting to believe in the wisdom of that phrase.

BODY COMPOSITION

The proportion of body fat and fat free mass in the body is referred to as Body Composition. This is important to understand, because most of us judge our body mass by standing on a bathroom scale—trust me—the scale is STUPID! I could show you two people who were the same height and the same weight and you would say that one was normal, and the other was fat, and you would be right. In order to find out body composition, there are some methods that are commonly used: skin fold calipers, bioelectrical impedance, BMI, and under water weighing.

A normal body composition range for a woman is approximately 25% body fat while a male is 18%. Having too much fat on our bodies is a condition called obesity and typically starts when a woman is over 30% and a male is over 25%. Obesity puts us at risk for many diseases, including heart disease, certain cancers and Type Two Diabetes.

Exercise is important to help keep our body composition in a healthy range, but diet becomes much more important as we age. In other words, we can't just work out and eat junk and processed foods anymore like we did when we were younger. We need both a lifestyle exercise plan and a healthy eating plan. They go together like puzzle pieces. Without one of these pieces, your overall health will always have a giant abyss that no medication will ever fill.

So remember, that you cannot store fitness, and if you haven't exercised in a while, you might have to start over again. For those of us who do exercise, we need to make sure we stay motivated so we can continue to enjoy the benefits that an active lifestyle brings. Unfortunately, many people who start an exercise program, quit in as little as six months, usually because they expect the fast results. It took us a while to get to where we are now and it's going to take a while to change so we just have to be patient. Here are some tips to keep you motivated on How to Stay Fit For Life!

1. Make the commitment to exercise for yourself. You should want to do this for you and you alone. No one else should enter this picture.

2. Pick the activities that you enjoy; go for the fun things first.

3. When you are working out, enjoy the moment. Keep any negative thoughts out of your mind when you are working out. This is YOUR time! As I tell my fitness students—don't bring your psychic trash into the gym.

4. Variety beats boredom. Add new exercises and activities periodically to spice up your workout.

5. Replace negative incentives with positive ones. Focus on what you want instead of what you don't want.

6. Make excuses to be more active instead of less active. Walk whenever you can. Take the stairs instead of the elevator.

7. On occasion, listen to audio books while you do a cardio workout or walk. Self-improvement tapes will not only make the time go faster, but will kill two birds with one stone. You get the physical along with the mental.

8. For some activities, a workout partner can help you get motivated. You might find a reason why you don't feel like working out, but if someone is waiting on you, you are more inclined to go because of your commitment to your "buddy."

9. Reward yourself for your efforts--perhaps a massage or a new article of clothing when you reach one of your goals.

10. Set both long term goals and mini goals. This will keep you moving forward.

11. Exercise outside as much as possible. Sunlight tends to improve mood.

12. Get enough sleep. You are more likely to have energy to work out when you are well rested.

13. Pick a role model that you know and ask for lifestyle advice. What works for them? Use what makes sense to you.

14. Stay off the scale. If fact, if you have the guts, throw it away. Instead focus on how you feel and how your clothes fit.

15. Join a team of fit individuals. There are several walking groups and active senior organizations.

16. See yourself as a fit individual and live that part. Your mind will work toward that image.

17. Avoid negative people who do not support your fit lifestyle. They are sometimes jealous because they are too lazy to work out and want to sabotage your efforts so they have more company in the "over the hill, unfit society."

18. Remember to progress slowly and wait for your body to adapt before you add more intensity.

Remember that exercise is not a punishment. It's a joy, a reward and should be fun. We are lucky to be able to do it, and I can guarantee you that once you commit to an active lifestyle that your whole life will change in a positive, phenomenal way. Enjoy your workouts, progress slowly and make exercise a priority for the rest of your life.

CHAPTER SIX

NUTRITION: YOUR NEW SUPERPOWER

"Perhaps no one realizes how important a good diet has been for me. I can't describe how important it is. You go along for years weighing too much. Then you change your diet, you start feeling good and you don't even mind looking in the mirror. Gradually, you rise to a different physical and mental level. It reflects on all your life, not just on your ability as an athlete."

—Jack Nicklaus

I LOVE SUPERHEROES AND OFTEN THOUGHT HOW AMAZING IT WOULD be to have some of those incredible powers. My favorite superhero was Wonder Woman, and I often watched the show with my two- year- old daughter. She was strong, sweet, and could kick anyone's butt if the person deserved it. I'm talking about Wonder Woman, not my daughter. I often tried to channel her when I was playing beach volleyball, especially against some of the competitors who acted like complete jerks on the court. There was one competitor, I'll just call her "The Queen", who not only played the game with fierceness and skill, but would also harass her competitors and even the crowd. Most people who competed against her were totally taken out of their game because they were so distracted and not prepared to deal with the continual onslaught of comments and antics. Let's just say, she added a new layer to the challenges of the sport.

Nutrition is the new layer in the aging game that is crucial to our health and vitality. Yet it is an area that many people ignore when it comes to dealing with aging challenges and do not realize what a powerful influence food has on our health. The food we eat can either increase our risks for all the chronic diseases or diminish our risk. The choice is ours. The exciting news is that some foods can even help our bodies heal and can be more effective than some medications in treating disease.

When we were younger, most of us didn't really think about our diet unless we were trying to lose weight. We just ate whatever was available, cheap and yummy. If you were an athlete, you most likely ate sensibly before your competitions, but the rest of the time, you probably ate a lot of high calorie junk food and didn't notice any adverse effects.

Well, guess what? As we enter the second half of life, we can't get away with that anymore. For one thing, we aren't training at the same intensity for the same amount of hours, and most likely our metabolism has slowed down. Athletes like Michael Phelps are burning up to 5,000 to 10,000 calories a day while training for their sport, so they can get away with eating large amounts of food. But when the training stops for the high level competitions, sometimes the eating habits do not change and these former athletes can become almost unrecognizable in just a few years.

I hate to admit it, but that happened to me a while back. I was one of those lucky people who could eat anything I wanted and never worried about gaining weight. I was active and busy and was blessed with a high metabolism. However, once I entered my forties, the game changed. I was putting on weight slowly and didn't even notice. I just thought my clothes had shrunk in the wash, and when I went shopping for new ones, that the sizes were somehow wrong. This went on for years, until one day, I saw a picture that had been taken at my sister's wedding. I thought someone else was wearing my dress, but it was ME in the picture, with a body that was unrecognizable - was it really me? Had my butt really gotten that big?

I immediately did the worst thing, I asked my dear husband Pat if he thought I was fat. Just so you know, my husband is incapable of lying. He took a deep sigh, looked away for a second, and then put his hand on my shoulder and said the unthinkable. "Yes, but I love you anyway and think you are beautiful." OUCH! I just wanted to smack him. But I immediately went into the bathroom and stepped on the scale that I had avoided for so long. I gently stepped on one foot at a time, closed my eyes, then opened them and saw my weight. I almost passed out.

So I know what it is like to struggle with weight. I always thought I was active enough to keep the weight off, but with my knee issues and not playing professional volleyball anymore, I wasn't working at the intensity I used to, but I was eating the same as I always had---anything I wanted. My husband gently shared a piece of advice he heard a while back from Chuck Norris... before 40 it's all exercise, after 40 it's all diet. It was time for me to clean up my act!

What's interesting is that healthy nutrition is not hard to understand, but in our society, it's hard to accomplish because of all the unhealthy choices that surround us. The next time you drive your car, count how many fast food places you see. I'll bet you can't go for two miles in a city without seeing at least one McDonalds. When you walk into a grocery store, take a look at all the processed foods that are full of sugar and chemicals. These food-like products are usually packaged to entice you to buy them with colors, false claims, and pictures.

When you watch TV, how many ads are there for foods that you know are unhealthy? Some of the ads equate their food with sex. Where else do you see people acting in these seductive behaviors when they are eating a hamburger? Unfortunately, food is a business and the food manufacturers don't care about your health. They care about money and will do whatever is necessary to get you to buy their products. Also, there are many supplements available that are said to reverse aging, and help you lose a ton of weight in a short time. Most of these are not only useless and don't work, but could also be dangerous.

So, it really is time to clean up our nutrition if we want to win at the aging game. Most of the conditions and challenges of aging are simply the long-term effects of poor nutrition catching up to us.

We also now know that certain foods can be harmful and put us at risk for the major killers, including heart disease, cancer, diabetes, autoimmune diseases and Alzheimer's. But instead of taking various medications that compensate and deal with symptoms of these conditions, doesn't it make sense to get to the cause instead and try to reverse or prevent the disease process?

Physically, our bodies are made up of cells that require both nutrients and oxygen to accomplish their various functions and also need to have toxins removed. This sounds easy, but most of the food we eat does not have various nutrients we need, especially some of the essential vitamins and minerals. However, the foods do have a lot of sugar and chemicals that the cells don't need. The extra sugar is stored as fat and plays havoc with our hormones, and the chemicals that the body cannot eliminate end up causing chronic inflammation.

I remember hearing about a little ten-year-old boy who was gaining a lot of weight and eating like crazy—he was always hungry! His mother took him to the doctor because she thought he might have a brain tumor. The doctor examined him, but before he ordered any tests, he asked what the boy was eating. His mom recited a litany of processed foods and fast foods—chips, cupcakes, donuts, cereal, cookies, French fries, hot dogs and so on. Thankfully, the doctor realized that the boy was not getting the nutrients he needed for his growing bones and muscles, and that's why he was so hungry! His brain was counting the nutrients, not the calories, and had the strong message for the boy to eat MORE! The doctor told the mom to start adding fresh fruits and vegetables and whole grains, and clean proteins to his diet—in other words—to *crowd out* the junk foods. The boy started to lose the fat, grew 4 inches, and stopped binging.

As you are most likely aware, the science of nutrition is full of controversy and contradictions. It is one of the few sciences where "the experts" don't seem to agree on much of anything. Is dairy healthy or harmful? Are all calories created equal? Can we really balance energy input and energy output? Do we need to eat everything organic? Are GMO's really harmful? Is a vegan diet healthy for everyone? Is caffeine harmful or can it be actually good for the brain? Do we need to drink alkaline water? Should we all be taking vitamins?

With all of these questions and contradictions, the concept of bio-individuality is especially important in putting together a healthy diet for each and every person. We are all different in our genetics, lifestyle, activities, where we live, blood types, personalities, biological functioning, hormone levels, preferences, conditioning and chronological age. What is healthy for one person could be poison for another. When my husband was taking Warfarin for his DVT's, he was not allowed to eat dark green leafy vegetables because Vitamin K, found in these foods, is a natural clotting factor. I couldn't believe it! I always thought at least green leafy vegetables were healthy for everyone. But I was wrong.

Also, when I had an ALCAT test to determine food sensitivities, I was shocked to find out the #1 food that caused inflammation in my body was iceberg lettuce. Also, we know that some people can experience severe problems with dairy, gluten, shellfish and nuts while other people are fine eating these foods. So we need to understand that when it comes to nutrition and food, *one size does not fit all*. Now is the time to find the foods that fuel our lives, make us feel great and will help us stay healthy as we age.

Intuitively, we know what our bodies need and what they don't. We need to listen to our bodies, and realize that if we want to live a healthy life up to the end, we can no longer ignore the incredible power of food. Now it's vital that we make our health and life a priority by taking our nutritional needs seriously.

I'm not suggesting that we do an about-face and change everything at once. However, we can always start to replace our bad nutritional habits with good ones by crowding them out as the doctor suggested the mom do with her son. And doing something is always better than doing nothing. Also, the cool thing about nutrition is that each and every day of our lives can either be better or worse with the food we choose to eat that day. It you want to have a great day, eat great food!

Here are some nutritional strategies that you can put into practice. Again, these don't work for everyone, but they are worth trying.

1. Look at food with different lenses. Start looking at food as being your fuel for an energetic, vivacious, disease free life instead of a pleasurable indulgence or quick treat. We need to feed ourselves intentionally rather than impulsively. Before you put anything in your mouth ask yourself: "Why am I eating this food?" and "How will this make me feel 20 minutes after I eat it?"

2. Embrace your individuality when it comes to food. Cultivate body wisdom by both becoming aware of the foods that make you feel healthy and alive, and those that make you feel tired and sick. A food journal is a great way to monitor food changes along with how you feel and what symptoms you are experiencing. For example, if one of my students or clients has problems with digestion, energy, excess mucus production, and I see that they eat a lot of dairy, I'll suggest that they cut out dairy for a week and see how they feel. Sometimes, this works like magic!

3. Start adding more raw fruits and vegetables to your diet. Having a large salad with multiple veggies of all colors with a little vinaigrette or lemon juice is a great way to get vitamins, minerals and enzymes, and also dietary fiber.

4. Cut down or eliminate processed foods. One of my friends, Kevin, is in his 50's and still plays high-level beach volleyball and appears to be in his 30's. His secret? He never eats anything from a box or a bag.

5. Drink more water. This is the most important food we can consume. It is the one required medium for all the body's chemical reactions and also provides lubrication for circulation, digestion and excretion. An added benefit most people are not aware of is that water also suppresses the appetite, and helps the body metabolize stored fat. Drink at least six to eight glasses a day... more if you exercise. Don't wait until you are thirsty. You're eliminating water every day in sweat, respiration, and urination and that water needs to be replaced, or dehydration will set in. One of the first signs of dehydration is fatigue and muscle stiffness. Maybe instead of getting old, we're just dehydrated!

6. When you eat a meal, finish it a little hungry instead of totally satiated. Eat only when you are hungry and stop when you aren't hungry anymore. Trust me, you'll feel a lot better and have more energy. My dad used to always say—"Don't Gormadize!" Give your digestive system a chance to work. You wouldn't overload your washing machine, or it might break and the clothes wouldn't get clean. So why eat until you are stuffed? If you cup your hands together, that is the total size of a normal stomach.

7. Organic foods have not been sprayed with pesticides and as we get older, we want to cut down on ingesting chemicals in our foods. The following produce usually contains the most residues in terms of pesticides and are known as the Dirty Dozen: Apples, Strawberries, Celery, Peaches, Spinach, Nectarines Grapes, Bell Peppers, Potatoes, Blueberries, Lettuce and Kale. These are in order from the most contaminated to the least. For these foods, I always suggest buying them organic if possible.

The foods with the lowest levels of residues, also known as The Clean 15 are: Onions, Corn, Pineapple, Avocado, Asparagus, Sweet Peas, Mangoes, Eggplant, Cantaloupe, Kiwis, Cabbage, Watermelon, Sweet Potatoes, Grapefruit and Mushrooms. This produce ranking was developed by analysts at the Environmental Working Group and is based on nearly 51,000 tests for pesticide residues on produce collected from the U.S. Department of Agriculture between 2000 and 2009.[1] Since buying organic products is more expensive, it makes sense to make sure to know which produce tends to have the most pesticides and which ones have the least. I always tell my students to try to buy the Dirty Dozen organic if they can, especially apples which are first on the list.

8. When you buy produce, whether it is a fruit or a vegetable, there is a label on each piece called a PLU. This helps the person scan the product when you check out. Next time you buy produce, look at the label. Conventionally grown produce that has been sprayed with pesticides has a four digit code that either starts with a 3 or a 4. Organic produce has usually a five-digit number that starts with a nine, and genetically modified fruits and vegetables have a five-digit number that begins with an 8. If you are concerned about GMO's, don't eat produce that has a PLU that starts with an 8. My students freaked out when they went to the store and found out how many products had an 8 at the start of the PLU, especially the grapes. While the verdict is not out yet as to what extent GMO's can affect our health and longevity, I know that I want to stay away from them as much as possible.

9. If you eat meat, look for grass-fed, certified organic and local whenever possible. Be picky about your protein! You don't really need that much in your diet, as most adults get way more than their body needs, which can cause kidney problems. Also, if you love salmon, choose wild or Atlantic salmon whenever possible. The farmed salmon is always cheaper, but these poor fish spend their lives in crowded pools and eat corn feed—is that normal? Also, some of them get diseases because of the overcrowding and others are given hormones to get them bigger. Also, in some of these farms, the fish are being genetically modified. So wild is

more expensive, but worth it when you consider your overall health. Salmon is one of the healthiest foods, so make sure it stays that way in your diet and isn't tainted.

10. Eat slowly and chew your food. Put down your fork in-between bites and really enjoy what the food tastes like. Some people eat so fast it's like they are shoving food into a trashcan. Eating should be enjoyable and foods need to be chewed thoroughly in order to be digested properly.

11. Sit down to eat. And I'm not talking about eating in your car. You're really not that busy, are you? Plan your meals and sit down and turn off the television. Be mindful about eating. I remember one party where there was a ton of food and when we were cleaning up, one of the ladies said, "Where did all the chips go?" As we asked around, it became apparent that SHE had eaten all the chips, and didn't even know it. She was talking and eating at the same time, and didn't even realize that she had consumed over 1,000 calories.

12. Try the 80/20 approach to eating. Eat what you know is healthy 80% of the time and save 20% for the foods that you know are not-so-nourishing. Or you can try using the 90/10 approach which is even better. However, don't try to be perfect with eating. Instead of going for the A+, go for the B+. We only live once, and we should be able to have treats now and then. If we can't, it's normal for us to want to have something that we are told we can't have. If you told me that I could never have a Big Mac again in my life, then I would want one. Obviously there is no such thing as the food police, so it's up to us to utilize the principle of moderation. When I see other people's cart in the checkout line at the grocery store, it's more than obvious that most people are using the 80/20 principle the opposite way. They are eating unhealthy food 80% of the time and healthy food 20% of the time, if that.

13. Be careful when eating out at restaurants. Most of the popular restaurants have nutritional information available that list the calories, fat and fiber content. I like to check out the nutritional information online before we go to a restaurant, because when we are ordering, sometimes we feel rushed and might choose differently if we didn't have this information ahead of time.

Here is my list of the top ten foods that you might want to add to your daily diet to help defy the aging process and enable you to feel great at any age. This is my personal list of foods because I know that they are nutrient dense, are loaded with antioxidants, have fiber, are filled with vitamins and minerals, are low on the glycemic index, have healthy fats, improve memory, contain anti-inflammatory properties, stimulate metabolism and also taste great! Obviously there are many foods that have these properties, so my list is just a sample.

1. BLUEBERRIES.

The Queen of the berries! These small, beautiful, blue treasures are power packed with anti-aging properties. I remember seeing an episode on Dr. Oz where he did an assessment on a woman to determine her real age. (A fun assessment you can take online at www.realage.com) This woman was in her mid- forties and the real age test came back with her assessed age being in her 60's. He explained the reasons for the score, with several medical assessments and lifestyle choices she had made. Then he told her how to reverse her score. One of the things he did was to give her a bowl of blueberries, and I remember her eating them slowly with a hopeful look on her face.

I know that blueberries will not reverse your age by twenty years all by themselves, but when you look at the properties these gifts from Mother Nature provide, it certainly would be an easy food to add to your diet.

Here are some of the properties in blueberries: High in antioxidants, enhances disease fighting capabilities, low calorie, low glycemic, high in fiber, helps with memory, reduces stomach fat, helps with motor function skills, packed with iron, manganese, and vitamins C and E. The cool thing about blueberries is that you can eat them by themselves or add them to yogurt, oatmeal, a shake and even a salad. The only addendum I would add, is to make sure you buy them organic. They are high on the Dirty Dozen List. Also, all berries are nutritious, so adding them to your diet for most people is beneficial.

2. Avocados

It's a fruit! It's a vegetable! It's an avocado! I still haven't figured out if it is a fruit or a vegetable, but what I know for sure, is that it is one of Mother Nature's treasures, even if it does look like a crinkled up, rough, soft, dark green oblong object. It's like one of those guys who doesn't necessarily have the great looks or body and sometimes doesn't stand out with women who are looking for the chiseled Adonis. But it's what inside that counts. The avocado is full of healthy monounsaturated fats that are important for every cell in the body, especially the brain. It also has protein, B vitamins, antioxidants and vitamin E. Some of its properties include soothing inflammation, preventing wrinkles, and increasing fat metabolism. Plus, it is smooth and yummy and can be added to most other foods, even shakes! The only problem is that you can have too much of a good thing. Even though the fat is a healthy fat, it still has 9 calories per gram, so don't overeat them. However, you don't have to buy them organic. They are on the Clean 15 list.

3. Coconut Oil

When I first heard about the benefits of coconut oil, I didn't believe it because it is loaded with saturated fat. However, this saturated fat is considered healthy because of the make-up of the fatty acids. Coconut oil is arranged in medium chain fatty acids, not the long chains of most of the animal products that contain saturated fats. The medium chain fatty acids are smaller than the long chains and are easily digested and immediately converted to energy. Coconut oil also has lauric acid that has antiviral properties, and there are a lot of viruses lurking around us each and every day we interact with other people. It is a great option for cooking since it doesn't turn rancid at high heat like other oils. Also, it is a great moisturizer for the skin and can be used for your hair. It's also inexpensive and can be found everywhere. Plus, who doesn't like the taste and smell of coconut? Okay, my husband doesn't like it, but I do. It reminds me of being in Tahiti.

4. WILD SALMON

I love fish, and when I go to a restaurant, that is what I usually order because of all the unique ways it is prepared. However, my favorite is salmon, because no matter how you prepare it, it always tastes great. Even just grilled with lemon juice is awesome. I love the fact that salmon are such amazing specimens as they can survive in both fresh water and salt water and swim amazing distances in their lifetimes. Salmon provides a heart healthy source of protein plus Omega 3's. Omega 3's are another source of healthy fats, especially for the brain, that have been known to prevent cancer, improve memory, and help prevent Parkinson's disease. It is also a great source of Vitamin D, one of the essential vitamins that most American's do not get enough of. As I mentioned before, try to buy wild salmon, especially if you eat a lot of it. Farmed salmon is cheaper, but these poor fish don't get to swim anywhere, and are surrounded by unclean water and live in crowded conditions. Also, they are given antibiotics, and sometimes hormones to make them bigger. Also, some salmon has coloring added to it to make it look fresher. Don't settle for less. Buy wild, Copperhead, or Atlantic salmon whenever you can.

5. WHOLE GRAINS

I know that some people have decided to take all grains out of their diet, but I would caution against that. You do not want to deal with the problems that lack of fiber can bring to your life. Hello constipation and hemorrhoids. I remember seeing a video at a workshop where the moderator was discussing the need for fiber in our diets and how most Americans do not get close to enough. The recommendation is between 25 and 35 grams a day. Most people are lucky to get 15, which is not even close. The video was an autopsy of a male who had died, and the cause of death was unknown. He was a very large man, and when they opened up his colon, it became apparent as to what caused his death. A huge blockage had occurred. In fact, he had over 70 pounds of fecal material stuck in his colon. They called this condition FOS. When I discuss this with my health class I ask them what they think these initials might stand for. They usually get it right. It is an acronym for Full Of __hit.

Then we discuss why we need fiber in our diet and how hard it is to get unless we have a diet that has fruit, vegetables and whole grains. The combination of the three is usually the best way to meet the requirement because most people don't eat enough fruit and vegetables. If my students are any indication, I can say that with certainty.

Why whole grains? Because they still have all the fiber and vitamins and minerals intact. They have not been taken out to make the product white or a light brown and soft and light. Don't make the mistake of choosing refined, fortified or multi-grain. Most of these products don't have the nutrients and the fiber necessary for colon health. And as you have probably heard, most diseases start in the colon.

There are many whole grain choices, and you don't have to choose wheat, especially if you are sensitive to gluten. Oats and quinoa are excellent choices that taste great and are easy to include in your diet. I love having oatmeal in the morning, and have a favorite from Trader Joe's, Steel Cut Oatmeal, that is easy to prepare in the microwave. It's full for fiber, delicious, fast, and tastes great with a little almond milk or regular milk, and you can add nuts, seeds, and any fruit you like. What a great way to get your fiber, vitamins, minerals, and start your day!

As I tell my students, the next time you tell someone that they are FOS, you are probably right. Don't be one of those people. If you don't like any grains, and won't eat them, make sure you take a fiber supplement.

6. VEGETABLES

Okay. I was never really a fan of vegetables. When I was young, I used to feed my vegetables to Pepe, who I knew hid under our dinner table. He ended up being a healthy, happy dog and outlived most other dogs in his breed. (Cockapoo) Plus, he used to chase cars and had more energy than all of us combined. Maybe it was the vegetables he got every night from those of us at the table that didn't like them.

Well, now vegetables are my new best friends. The cool thing about vegetables is that they can be eaten raw or cooked, plain or endowed with spices and sauces, and are the perfect accompaniment for any meat. In fact, you probably would not even need any meat if you ate more vegetables since many of them have most of the essential amino acids, which are the building blocks of protein. However, not everyone can be a vegan.

When I was studying nutrition at the Institute for Integrative Nutrition, the one consistent food that was mentioned as being important to include in all the 100 diets I studied was vegetables. In fact, most of the eating plans suggested that at least half of our dietary intake each day should be vegetables. So, it's time to put them into our diet. There are many types of vegetables, but most of them are high in nutrients including antioxidants, vitamins and minerals, low in calories and high in fiber. They are also low on the glycemic index, which means that they are digested slowly and do not cause a fast rise in insulin like so many of our processed foods.

Get creative with vegetables! You can add them to a smoothie, omelet, sandwich, salad, casserole, stir-fry or as a meal. They can be eaten raw, cooked, steamed, baked, put in a crock- pot, and the list goes on. My favorites are anything green, and carrots and tomatoes and my all-time favorite, sweet potatoes! YUM! Just cut them up and put them on a cookie sheet in the oven, bake for 20-30 minutes and add some coconut or olive oil and sea salt. So much better than French fries!

7. GREEK YOGURT

I am not a dairy fan, because eating most dairy products makes me feel bloated and uncomfortable. However, I do love Greek Yogurt and try to have it at least a couple of times a week, especially after a workout. It is a great source of protein and calcium, and also is loaded with probiotics also known as "the good bacteria." These microorganisms live in our intestines and keep us healthy and also prevent too much bad bacteria from building up that can damage our immune systems and cause digestive problems, such as irritable bowel syndrome. It is also great source of vitamin B12, which is necessary for energy and brain health.

It is thicker and creamier than regular yogurt because it is strained three times or more instead of two to remove the whey. It's lower in carbohydrates than regular yogurt, which makes it a good choice for people with blood sugar problems.

The only caution, it to make sure and check the label, because Greek Yogurt tends to have a bland taste, and to compensate, many brands add a lot of sugar to make it taste better. Buy the unflavored type without the added fruit at the bottom. You can add your own fruit to sweeten it the way you like, and also some nuts or seeds. I love to add Greek Yogurt to my post workout shakes to give them a creamy, thicker consistency and also know that I am getting the protein I know my muscles need to recover. It seems to shorten my recovery time, especially after doing my soft sand sprints. Trust me, I need something to help me recover after doing those monsters.

The last three foods have health benefits, but must be consumed in small amounts because even though they are power packed with nutrients, they are also loaded with calories and can even be addicting.

8. NUTS

A cupped handful is one serving, not two handfuls. I must admit, I'm one of those people who can get carried away with nuts. The health benefits are many, including reducing the risk of heart disease and lowering the bad cholesterol, or LDL in the bloodstream. They are also chock full of Omega 3's, protein, and antioxidants, fiber and many vitamins and minerals.

However, they are also high in calories and contain 9 calories for every gram of healthy fat. So they are not a good food to binge on. I see them sold in large packages at the store, and sometimes bring in the packages and ask my students how many servings are in one of these packages. Most of them say one or two, when it is usually five or six, and sometimes more. Also, nuts are sometimes "enhanced" in mixtures, such as trail mix with dried fruit and chocolate. Even though these are yummy, they are very high in calories and sugar, and most people are just not aware. So be moderate with nuts. There are many types, and all of them are nutritious. My favorites are almonds, walnuts and macadamia nuts. They are Mother Nature's gifts that need to be savored, not engorged. You can mix them yourself and put them in small packages and take them with you for snacks, or stores like Trader Joe's sells them in a big bag with several small packages inside already measured for one serving. These are great to have with you at all times, especially when driving. Eat them slowly, because they will satisfy your appetite and probably prevent you from driving through a fast food place on the way home.

9. DARK CHOCOLATE

What a great way to rationalize eating chocolate. Who knew that chocolate could actually be good for you? The variety of chocolate that has the most health benefits is Dark Chocolate and is different from milk chocolate because it does not contain milk solids and definitely does not taste as sweet. However, there are many benefits from having a little bit each day or even a couple times a week. It has been shown to lower blood pressure and may also prevent the formation of blood clots, so it does help prevent heart disease. It is also good for your brain because it increases blood flow to the brain and can help improve cognitive function and may reduce the risk of strokes. However, the one benefit that most of us, especially women know intuitively, is that it makes you feel happier. That's because chocolate contains phenylethylamine (PEA) which is the same chemical your brain makes when you feel like you're falling in love. I've never met a woman who didn't like chocolate.

It can also help to prevent type 2 diabetes because the flavinoids in dark chocolate help reduce insulin resistance and it is also low on the glycemic index, which means it won't cause spikes in blood sugar levels. It is full of antioxidants that help neutralize free radicals, which can protect us from some types of cancer and slow aging symptoms. It is also high in many vitamins and minerals, including potassium, copper, iron and magnesium.

So, dark chocolate is more than just a guilty pleasure. It is a health food that must be consumed in small amounts in order to be beneficial. Just one 1.6 ounce of chocolate a day is all you need. I'm sure you're familiar with the saying, "An apple a day keeps the doctor away." How about changing that to "A dark chocolate a day keeps the doctor away." So cool!

10. RED WINE

As with nuts and dark chocolate, red wine does have some health benefits, but only in small amounts. Why is red wine healthier than white wine? The reason is because red wine is high in antioxidants, especially resveratrol, which comes from grape skins and seeds. Resveratrol may help prevent cancer by limiting tumor growth and also be good for your heart by raising the good cholesterol (HDL) and reducing the formation of blood clots. Obviously, there are other ways to reduce the risk of heart disease, so it is not recommended to start drinking red wine just to prevent heart disease. The research is still conflicting and drinking too much alcohol causes liver damage, certain cancers, high blood pressure and can weaken the heart muscle. So, it is recommended to either drink red wine in moderation, or not at all. For healthy adults, that means one drink a day for women and up to two drinks a day for men. One serving is considered 5 ounces.

That's my list of favorite foods, but there are many more that tastes great and have many health benefits. Find your 10 favorites that you know are healthy and that you enjoy eating, and add them to your diet.

The following foods are ones that we need to really stay away from if we are in the aging game. These foods have been known to increase risk of most of the major killers and also make us feel tired and cranky. Definitely NOT antiaging foods!

SUGAR

Even our government came out recently with new eating guidelines saying that we need to limit our sugar consumption to 10% of our diet. That wouldn't be hard if we were just eating table sugar and adding it to our coffee and baking goods. The problem is that sugar is in just about every processed food, such as catsup, yogurt, salad dressings, barbecue sauce, and even infant formula. Also, the food companies are aware that we know that if sugar is the first ingredient listed on the food label, that we should not eat it. However, many products now contain many different types of sugar and list them individually so none of them show up first. Some of them we don't even recognize as sugar such as: maltose, malt syrup, corn sweetener, fructose, dextrose, evaporated cane syrup and high fructose corn syrup. The most dangerous of these is fructose, because it is highly pro-inflammatory and tends to speed up the aging process.

The biggest sources of added sugars in our diet usually come from soft drinks and energy drinks. One 12-ounce can of Coke has at least 8 teaspoons of sugar. You would never sit down and eat 8 teaspoons of sugar or add that much to your cereal, but that's how much we take in with each and every can. No wonder the average America takes in over 130 pounds of sugar a year. It's just WAY too much!

So, one of the best things you can do with your diet, is to cut way down on any food that has high amounts of added sugar and high fructose corn syrup. You will be surprised at how much better you eventually feel, how much more energy you will have, and you might even lose some weight.

ARTIFICIAL SWEETENERS

Even though these don't have calories, they do have a lot of chemicals, some of which are totally foreign to the body. I do an experiment in my health class where I have some packets of sweeteners and will have a student come up to the front of the class to illustrate the immediate effect that some of these have on the body. It is called a muscle kinesiology test and is very easy to administer. I learned it from a Chinese holistic doctor and it usually makes a huge impact on my students. I usually pick out a strong person and have him or her stand facing the class. I stand in front of the student and ask him or her to extend their right arm straight in front or the shoulder. Then, I will try to push their arm down with the index and the middle finger of my right hand. I should not be able to do that and usually they keep their arm extended when I try to push it down.

Then I ask the student to close his or her eyes and I'll put a packet of an artificial sweetener in their extended hand. The one I always start with is aspartamine—the one in the pink packet. From just touching their wrist with my two fingers, most of their arms drop like a heavy weight. They immediately open their eyes and stare at the package. They can't believe it. I explain that energetically, the chemicals in the packet are not healthy for their bodies, and this is one way to find out which ones are the worst for them, and if any are okay. We test all the artificial sweeteners, honey, stevia, refined sugar, and raw sugar.

Remember that our bodies weren't designed to take in some of these chemicals that are in artificial sweeteners. They can be toxic to many people and put us at risk for cancer and autoimmune diseases. As we age, we should be cutting down on toxins that we ingest, not adding more. So switching to more natural sweeteners, such as honey or stevia are usually much better than the junk in the pink, yellow or blue packages. Also, stay away from diet soft drinks. They are loaded with chemicals, salt and colorings.

CURED MEATS

The World Health Organization recently came out with a warning saying that bacon, ham and sausages now rank alongside cigarettes as a major cause of cancer.[2] I don't think that this means that we need to stop eating these foods altogether, but is probably does indicate that we should cut back and choose other foods when possible. Hot dogs, and luncheon processed meats would also fall into this category. Darn it! I love having hot dogs at the Dodger games. Thank goodness I don't get to go that often.

With so much food available, people often ask me if they also need to take vitamins. That is different for every individual, so it really is hard to answer. Most of us though, because of our food supply and choices, could probably benefit from taking a multivitamin that contains the recommended daily intakes for most of the essential vitamins and minerals. After that, it really does depend on your lifestyle, activity levels, family history, medical history, gender and age. The supplements I often see that are recommended for people over 50 are Vitamin D and Omega 3's. These vitamins and essential fats are imperative for heart health and especially brain health. Just make sure they have been certified to ensure safety.

The bottom line is food matters in our everyday health and affects how we age. We cannot get away with eating poor foods anymore or we will pay the price. Making small changes can transfer to big results! So, take a look at your diet and see where you can make some positive changes. Start to crowd out the foods you know are not healthy for you with foods that your body needs. The simplest place to start is with natural whole foods. Mother Nature knows how to package foods in the perfect combinations of nutrients and fiber. Man-made foods or processed foods are poor substitutions for real food. So, make the shift and think about feeding your body for performance. Remember, you are taking on aging as a sport, and you need to eat to win!

CHAPTER SEVEN

TIME OUT!

"Mindfulness is a certain way of paying attention that is healing, that is restorative that is reminding you of whom you actually are so that you don't wind up getting entrained into being a human doing rather than a human being."

—Jon Kabat-Zinn

AS WITH MOST ATHLETES, COACHES AND PARENTS, I HAVE ALWAYS strived to attain goals that appeared out of reach. "Aim High" was my mantra. Seeing people succeed and working as a coach, teacher and taskmaster gave my life meaning. However, eventually, my stress levels started to climb off the charts and I felt like a pressure cooker ready to blow. My body's persistent signals to slow down and my soul's gentle whisper to take a time-out were ignored.

Thanks goodness I found yoga. One of my health students asked about yoga and if it could improve a person's quality of life. Caught off guard and dissatisfied with my lack of information, I set forth to do some research since I never practiced yoga or knew anyone who was an expert. My only clue was my husband's prized yoga book, with an emaciated man on the cover in a turban with his legs seemingly tied in knots.

Coincidentally, a new yoga studio had just opened in our town and it was offering incentives to attract new members. Since the studio was near, I signed up for a class and went the next day for my first yoga experience. I remember walking into the studio feeling like a fish out of water. The room was somewhat dark with strategically placed lights, soothing music, and there was an inviting sense of calm as you entered. People were either sitting quietly with their eyes closed, or talking in hushed voices. The class appeared to have people of all ages, sizes, and an equal amount of men and women. I took a mat out of the bin and immediately found a place in the back of the room. I was excited about the class, but also a little scared. I had no idea about what to expect.

Five minutes later, the music was turned off and a tall woman dressed in black walked into the room and in a soft voice introduced herself. She explained that we would move at a slow pace during class, listen to our bodies, not compete with anyone else, and rest whenever we wanted in a "child's pose." This was new to me. In sports, I was always taught to push through pain, compete at any cost and only rest if I was hurt.

The soft music came back on and we started, with some deep breathing exercises. Immediately, I was bored. Was it going to get more interesting? I soon found out. Even though my body was in decent shape I struggled through the class. What a revelation to find that my upper body was weaker than expected and that my shoulder and hip flexibility was sadly lacking. I felt like a foreigner in my own body. Out of the corner of my eye, I could see the other students moving effortlessly through the class as if it were a moving meditation. I could feel myself struggle as I tried to hit each pose with perfection. Finally, my body started to scream at me and I did the unthinkable, I hit the child's pose. My competitive nature was receiving a well-deserved beating.

The end of the class was what changed my life. We were told to lie on our backs and try to be still and come back to just noticing our breath. With my body still shaking from the practice, I couldn't even hold that pose and felt like a newly caught fish flopping around on the deck. Finally, I started to relax, and my overactive mind finally let go of my body. It was an incredible experience as I laid there, and I didn't even care that I was probably the worst student in the class that day. I just loved the feeling of relaxing, with nowhere to go and nothing to do but lie still and be with my breath. WOW!

I decided that I had to share this with others, especially people like me who say they don't need yoga, or relaxation techniques, but are probably the ones that need it the most. I now have over 2,000 hours of training and have been teaching yoga at the college for sixteen years. I love seeing stressed out students learn how to practice yoga, meditation and using breath to take well needed breaks from their busy lives.

In our fast paced society, the mind has been trained to analyze, criticize, compete, and compute... all in response to the outside environment. As a rule, Westerners are not encouraged or motivated to turn their thoughts inward for self-reflection. We are constantly directing our attention outward where our senses bring in constant information for us to process and act upon. Technology has enabled us to be even more tuned into the environment. We can't seem to turn off the noise except when we sleep, and sometimes, we can't even do that.

As an athlete, I remember being in competitions where nothing was going right, the other team was running up the score, and we were out of sync. It was such a relief to hear our coach call a time out. Even though the time out wasn't for a long period, it was usually just long enough to give us a break, and reset us to get back on track. In the aging game, we can take time outs for as long as we want. And there are so many different types to choose from.

Many people retreat to a quiet place and listen to music or read an inspirational book. Some take a silent walk in a natural environment that is sometimes referred to as a walking meditation. Others have an actual meditation or visualization practice or a breathing practice. For people who love technology, there are several meditation programs online that include guided visualizations and instructions on how to meditate. However, if you love technology and want to try something really innovative, check out the emwave stress reduction tools from Australia at www.emwave.com. One of my friends calls it his "Yoga Machine." It is a personal stress reliever that measures the space between heartbeats and utilizes breathing and biofeedback to get into a stress free zone. It is compatible with any computer, iPhone or tablet and the best part is that it only takes 2 - 5 minutes a day in order to get the benefits. It is a little pricy, but if it works for someone where other stress management techniques fail, then it is more than worth the price.

What is the price that we pay if we don't take time-outs? Does it surprise you to know that most diseases are caused at least in part by unresolved stress? The National Mental Health Association estimates that 70-90% of visits to doctors are stress related. The sympathetic nervous system puts us into a state called "fight or flight" when our survival is treated or danger is perceived. Our bodies automatically go into this heightened state, preparing to either fight for survival, or run away. This response served us well thousands of years ago, but today, we continue to activate this response but in most cases, are not allowed to act on it.

Whenever we encounter resistance to the fulfillment of our needs and desires, our minds and bodies become activated. Any threat to our safety, happiness, self-esteem, or health can provoke the fight or fight stress response. In other words, stress can be defined as how we respond to not having our needs met.

In the fight or flight response, the following physiological changes occur:

The heart rate increases

Blood pressure rises

Breathing is faster and shallow

Perspiration occurs

The adrenal glands secrete adrenaline, norepinephrine and cortisol

The pancreas releases more glucagon and less insulin resulting in elevated blood sugar

Blood supply is reduced to the digestive organs

Blood supply to the muscles increases

The immune system is suppressed

For obvious reasons, the body should only go into this state for emergencies threatening our survival. Flight or fight is damaging to the body if it is activated too often, especially if no action occurs. For example: suppressing the immune system can make us vulnerable for infections and cancer; elevated blood pressure and heart rate puts stress on the heart and increases the risk of heart attacks, the release of stress hormones increases the risks of anxiety and insomnia, consistently elevated blood sugar puts us at risk for diabetes, and decreased blood flow to the digestive organs may cause a whole host of digestive problems, including IBS.

Avoiding constant stimulation and stress in today's world is a challenge, especially with most people walking around with a cell phone. You should see the look on my students' faces when I tell them that they can't have their phones on their mats during yoga practice. It's like taking away their favorite pet. When I mention meditation, a lot of my students start thinking that I'm going to make them do something demanding, hard and weird. But they are very surprised to find out that meditation is really a process of inner exploration or a state of restful awareness. It is the perfect anecdote to the sensory overload we all experience and the stress that comes with it. Imagine your mind is the floor in the basement with dirt, feathers, dust and junk everywhere. Meditation is like a broom that sweeps away the debris, leaving a clean space.

According to Deepak Chopra, "Meditation takes us beyond the mental prison of doubt, anxiety and judgment to the silent field of expanded awareness in which we remember our essential nature as peaceful, centered and creative. Just a few minutes a day allows us to experience wholeness in our lives, which supports balance, healing and transformation."[1]

Dr. Benson substituted the phrase "Relaxation Response" for Meditation in order to demystify the process for the general population. According to Dr. Benson "The relaxation response is a physical state of deep rest that changes the physical and emotional responses to stress.... and the opposite of the fight or flight response."[2] However, it doesn't really matter what you call it because it is the perfect time-out and doesn't take long at all.

So how does meditation or the relaxation response work in helping us manage stress? Meditation activates the parasympathetic nervous system which has the opposite effects of the sympathetic system. During meditation, the body shifts into a state of restful awareness, which counterbalances the fight or flight response. For this reason, it is the perfect antidote for a stressful life. Here are some of the responses that occur when a person is in a state of meditation[3]

Heart rate slows down

Blood pressure goes down or normalizes

Breathing slows down

Less perspiration, if any

Adrenal glands produce less adrenaline, norepinephrine and cortisol

The body makes more sex hormones, especially DHEA

Your pituitary gland releases more HGH, or human growth hormone (An anti-aging hormone)

Your immune system improves

For some people, meditation is an easy practice, but for others, it is easier said than done. Many people have trouble sitting down, closing their eyes and focusing on breathing while quieting the mind. I remember my first 30 minute meditation exercise at the Chopra Center where I was taking a meditation workshop. 30 minutes seemed like an eternity, and after about 10 minutes, I was ready to run out of the room. However, I stayed and after doing this three times a day, by the end of the week 30 minutes in meditation seemed like 3 minutes. So if you want to try meditation, be patient with yourself because it might require several attempts. Once you get into a consistent meditative practice, it becomes as much of a part of your day as eating, sleeping, exercising or brushing your teeth. A rule of thumb is to not have any expectations. Every experience may be different.

If you want to start a meditation practice on your own, here are some tips: If you get frustrated, there are many programs and classes in your community and online which are helpful. Remember that we are all different, and what works for one person may not work for another.

1. Establish a space for your meditation practice. It doesn't have to be a large space since you are the only person who will be there. However, the area must be clean, comfortable and appealing. You should want to go there, so it's helpful to create some special effects, such as a picture plant candle or low lights. Some people like to have a comfortable blanket, pillow or cushion that is only used for meditation. Others like to use a favorite comfortable chair. If you don't have a space, meditation can be done anywhere, even outside in nature. I do mine everyday down by the ocean.

2. Make sure this space is quiet. Let your family and friends know that you need to be left alone for this time. Turn off the radio, television, phone or anything else that has the potential to disrupt your practice.

3. Make meditation a routine. Make it the same time each day or night so it becomes a habit. You only need to schedule five to ten minutes at the start and eventually work up to thirty minutes.

4. Prepare for your meditation. Just as you would calm down a young child before you left for a while, in order to reduce anxiety, you should give your mind some preparation before you

meditate. Play some soothing music, light some candles, turn the lights down or do some light yoga or progressive relaxation techniques to get your body ready to be still.

5. Start your meditation seated. You can sit in any position as long as the back is straight. Some people sit in a chair or against the wall for extra support. However, you should not lie down because instead of meditating, you might fall asleep.

6. Close your eyes and tune into your body and breath. Start to lengthen the breath and notice the sensations of inhaling and exhaling. Continue observing the breath until you start to feel calm. You might find yourself struggling at first with your mind wandering off like a spoiled child who wants to do its own thing. A to-do-list might pop up with urgency. These things are normal. Keep coming back to your breath and stay until you feel a calming effect. When your mind reaches this point, enjoy the stillness and silence for as long as you like.

7. Sometimes, during a meditation, people experience insights or breakthroughs. It's a good idea to have a pen or pencil available and a notebook when you finish. Sometimes the jewels that we uncover in a meditation can change our lives. Write them down so you don't forget.

There are many types of meditation, some challenging, and others incredibly easy. Most meditation practices fall into one of three categories; Exclusive, Inclusive and Mindfulness.

In Exclusive Meditation, the focus is on the breath, a mantra or sometimes an object. When a distracting thought enters the mind, you are encouraged to go back to the focus. Transcendental Meditation has been taught by Maharishi Mahesh Yogi since 1958, and is easy to learn, but must be individually taught. This technique has over 600 research studies that show extensive health and emotional benefits. If you are interested go to www.tm.org and research instructors in your area.

Another easy to learn technique is Primordial Sound Meditation from the ancient Vedic traditions of India. Dr. Chopra revived this technique in 1995 and made it available in a format that anyone can learn. The mantras, or primordial sounds, are used as tools to interrupt the flow of thoughts, allowing our attention to expand to a deeper level of awareness, and eventually to silence. If you want to get an individualized mantra based on your time of birth, you will have to go to a Primordial Sound Meditation teacher. The Chopra Center has Primordial Sound Meditation classes, workshops and instructor training. This is where I went to learn meditation, and I have my own mantra. If you would like to try this type of meditation, there is a simple technique I teach to my yoga students and most of them find it easy to do, and very effective. Once you become seated and start to slow down your breathing, say to yourself "SO" on the inhale, and "HUM" on the exhale. Breathe in and out through your nose. Continue the process for 2 - 5 minutes the first time. As it becomes easier, try to extend your time, eventually to 30 minutes.

Some of my students prefer Inclusive meditation, where it is almost like you are watching yourself think. As easy exercise is to imagine your thoughts as logs floating down a stream and you are standing on the shore watching them go by. You don't attach any meaning or feeling to the thoughts or judge them. You just let each thought float by and then wait for the next one. When we do this in my class, some of my students notice that the thoughts stop coming and they are in a place of complete relaxation.

Finally, Mindfulness Meditation is a type that you can do anywhere, anytime, and you don't have to be seated. It involves being completely aware of the present moment. Most of the time, when we feel stressed, our attention is in the past or the future, not the present moment. Jon Kabat-Zinn has been instrumental in bringing mindfulness into the mainstream of medicine, health care, professional sports and corporations. Says Kabat-Zinn: "Mindfulness is a certain way of paying attention that is healing, that is restorative, that is reminding you of whom you actually are so that you don't wind up getting entrained into being a human doing rather that a human being."[3] You can easily practice this the next time you eat a meal by becoming completely aware of how the food tastes, the texture, the temperature and the sensations of chewing and swallowing. It really is interesting to try.

One of my favorite ways to take a time out is to do a guided visualization. It's also easy, because all you have to do is sit or lie still, and listen to the directions. My yoga students love doing these because they are fun, and really take them to another place. There are several resources available if you want to try them. Here is one that I do in my class from Brian Seaward. It involves visualization and breathing. It's called the "Breathing Cloud Meditation".[4]

1. Begin by closing your eyes and focusing on your breath.

2. Now, as you take your next breath—slowly and comfortably inhale through your nose and imagine you are inhaling clean, fresh air, like a white puffy cloud. Feel the air circulate up through your sinuses, up to the top of your head, and down the back or your spine.

3. As you begin to exhale, slowly and comfortably exhale through your mouth. As you exhale, visualize that the air you exhale if a dark, dirty cloud of air. As you exhale, bring to your mind a thought or feeling that no longer serves you and let it go as you exhale.

4. Inhale again, clean fresh air through your nose. Let it circulate to the top of your head and down the back of your spine to where it resides in your stomach.

5. Exhale very slowly through your mouth, and as you do, think of a moment of frustration or feeling of resentment that you have been holding onto for a while. Now is the time to let it go. As you exhale, visualize the dark, dirty air you breathe out carrying this toxic thought as it leaves with the breath.

6. Continue inhaling through the nose visualizing a white cool cloud and exhale through your mouth visualizing a dark cloud leaving your body along with tension and negativity.

I paraphrase this exercise for my students, guide them at the start, and then let them continue on their own. Brian's book, *Health of the Human Spirit*, has several of these guided visualizations, and my students love them. He also has them on DVD's. [4]

Have you ever tried to relax your body and didn't even know where to begin? If so, a Progressive Relaxation practice calms the body one part at a time and is an easy technique that can be done anywhere. It's a relatively easy technique to learn and can be done anytime. It can be used before going to sleep, at your office when you need a break, before meditation, or when you are waiting in the doctor's or dentist's office. You get the idea.

Here is a short guide: (Some people like to listen to soft music when they do this exercise)

1. Find a comfortable position either seated or lying down.

2. Close your eyes and start to become aware of your breathing.

3. Bring your awareness either to the top of the head or the feet.

4. Either tense that part of the body and then relax it, or imagine a light shining on that part of the body and feel a warming sensation in that body part.

5. Feel that part of the body become heavier as it relaxes.

6. Work your way up or down the body bringing your awareness to only one area at a time. Again, tense and relax the body part or imagine a light shining on that part that is bringing in warmth.

7. When you are done, notice a wave of relaxation as it moves through your entire body.

8. Finally, come back to noticing your breath and open your eyes slowly. You are now ready for that dentist!

Writing can be an effective stress management tool, and a form of meditation. Have you ever had a plethora of random worrisome thoughts and wrote them down, and found that your mind was quiet afterward? Or have you ever been so angry with someone that you wanted to confront them in an unsettled state, but instead wrote down your feelings and felt better as a result? If you are doing this on your computer, don't send it to the person. I learned this from experience.

ENTER THE POWER OF WRITING!

Many of us have an obsessive mind that causes anxiety, even though we are not doing anything to cause it. Thoughts of the past, or what might be coming at us in the future can get the best of us if we continue to let the excessive, negative, inner dialogue keep our attention. Why not write the thoughts down on paper and get them out of our heads? For most people, writing is a challenge because most of what we have written in the past has been edited, analyzed, criticized or graded. No wonder we feel uncomfortable! So, if you haven't discovered how powerful writing can be when dealing with stress, why not try it?

I attended a writing workshop at Esalen in Big Sur, California recently put on by Catherine Ann Jones, who is a playwright, screenplay writer, and author. I love to write, and wanted to learn from the best, and she did not disappoint. It was a week of creative writing, and I was in the company of some incredibly gifted writers and creative minds. Besides learning the craft of creative writing, she introduced us to her new book, *Heal Yourself With Writing*. We got to do some of the exercises from the book, and I think that was the most amazing part of the workshop. As we worked through the days, writing for hours on end, people began writing more about their personal lives and stories, and that's when the event became magical. Everyone has a story, including you! In the introduction to her book Catherine says: "Expressing and listening to one's story is an ancient mode of healing. There is an overwhelming need today for people to be heard, to tell their stories, to earn and grow from their experience both individually and collectively. It is crucial that we offer constructive and transformative methodology for this process. It may mean the difference between deep, transformative healing and some form of 'acting out' or self-destruction both personally and collectively." [5]

So I encourage you to write a little everyday even if it's just for a small amount of time. It is incredibly therapeutic and can be done by writing freestyle in a journal or guided as in Catherine's book, *Heal Yourself With Writing*. Who knows? If you really get into writing, your own life story could become a best seller or developed into a screenplay.

One of the most important time-outs we need every day for at least 7 - 8 hours is a restful sleep. For a lot of people, this is easy and they are out once their head hits the pillow. For others it is very difficult, and insomnia can have a radical effect on a person's well-being and health. Sleep deprivation has been shown to decrease the immune system, increase anxiety and accelerate aging. As we know, there are several over the counter sleep aids, but they are only a short-term solution. Over time they can lose their effectiveness, can cause dependence and have numerous side effects.

So how do you beat insomnia without taking drugs? For most people, the key is in preparation and routine. After a day of activity your body is ready for and needs deep sleep for recovery.

HERE ARE A FEW TIPS ON HOW TO PREPARE FOR A RESTFUL NIGHT'S SLEEP:

1. Avoid caffeine, tobacco and alcohol as much as possible, especially in the evening.

2. Eat a relatively light dinner no later than 7pm. Never go to bed on a full stomach.

3. Minimize exciting, aggravating or mentally intense activities after 8:30 pm. That includes anything that makes you feel stimulated, irritated, or tense.

4. Aim to be in your bed with the lights out before 10:30 pm. Since the most rejuvenating hours of sleep are before midnight, you don't want to miss out!

5. Use your bedroom only for relaxation and keep it cool, quiet, and somewhat dark. Make sure you have a comfortable mattress. If not, it may be time to splurge on a new one. Most mattresses wear out in 8 years or less.

6. Regularity and rhythm are important in establishing healthy sleep cycles. Try to go to sleep at the same time each evening and wake up at the same time in the morning.

7. About an hour before bedtime, run a hot bath and place a few drops of oil such as lavender, sandalwood or vanilla into the water. You can also massage these oils into your skin.

8. Listen to calm music while in the bath.

9. After your bath drink something warm such as a cup of warm milk with nutmeg and honey, or chamomile tea.

10. If your mind is still overly active, journal a few minutes before bed. This will create a downloading effect of thoughts so they are out of your head before you try to sleep.

11. Do no watch television or do work in bed.

12. Do not watch horror movies or crime movies right before bed. In fact, forget the news. Most of the time, it is upsetting and can activate your flight or fight response.

13. Once in bed, close your eyes and bring attention to your body and notice where you still feel tension and consciously relax that area.

14. If you still can't fall asleep, use a warm water bottle or heating pad and place it on your stomach. This helps to soothe the body and calm the mind.

15. You can also try a CD or stream some quiet soft music into your player.

So, the bottom line is that we all need time-outs. Getting a massage, manicure, reading a book or playing an instrument are also good choices to get the time we need to rejuvenate. As my Dad always says, "Slow down and smell the bees." I think he means the roses, but it's funnier when he says bees. Make sure you have some time-outs that work for you and do them often! Otherwise, you'll be spending your time-outs being sick in bed or in a hospital. Definitely, not the kind of relaxation response you want.

CHAPTER EIGHT

AGING IS A TEAM SPORT—BUILDING YOUR SUPPORT SYSTEM

"People acting together as a group can accomplish things which no individual acting alone could ever hope to bring about."

—*Franklin D. Roosevelt*

A WHILE BACK WE WENT TO A RESTAURANT IN JAPAN THAT HAD "FRESH lobster." However, this lobster was "over the top" fresh. You could view the big pot where the lobsters were being boiled alive. I was horrified as I watched these crustaceans scrambling about in the water, and when one of the brave ones tried to climb out of the pot, the other lobsters would reach up with their claws and pull the poor guy back into the pot. Needless to say, I didn't order lobster that night, but it did get me thinking not only about how cruel we are to some of earth's creatures, but also how we humans tend to pull others down to our levels when we are suffering. We don't want others to succeed if we can't or won't even try.

The reason I mention the lobster pot is because, unfortunately, Americans tend to have a fatalistic, negative view about aging. Our society tends to view the aging population as not having a productive role in society, is undeserving of respect, and that declining health is a certainty. I don't know about you, but I want OUT OF THE POT. I also need to find others who want out with me. Maybe we can even help those get out of the boiling water instead of giving up. We need to make some changes!

It's time to start putting together your team. When you were an athlete, you most likely were chosen for a team based on your skills and previous success in your sport. But the aging game is different. *We get to choose our own teams.* One of the best insights I ever got about understanding people is a quote my husband always says to me when I get frustrated and disappointed with some of the people in my life, "Limit your relationships to what you have in common." I consider this to be great advice.

As we go through various transitions in life, we tend to lose some people we used to have as friends and end up with others who share our new interests. Perhaps we don't change that much, but certainly our interests do, and how we choose to handle challenges. Think about how your life and relationships changed when you got that first full time job, or when you got married, moved, or started having kids. I'll bet some of the people who you thought would be your best buddies for life might have become distant or even disappeared. There just wasn't that much in common anymore. You certainly can't go out drinking with your buddies like you used to every night if you are now married, especially if you also have children.

The make-up of your team has several levels. The first and most important person on your team is YOU! In order to be successful at the Aging Game, you have to be *all in.* I'm sure you remember playing on some teams when you had people who just didn't seem to care that much, or who gave what I call "a half ass effort". Perhaps this person was you at the time, because you didn't really want to play the sport, didn't enjoy it, or someone else made you do it—like your parents.

But if you want to play this game, no one is forcing you. The goal here is not getting a trophy or a medal. It's about winning a high quality of life. So first of all, you have to realize that your life is valuable and you need to love and respect yourself. It's time to stop beating yourself up and realize how amazing you really are. The next time you look in the mirror, look into your own eyes and make a promise to yourself that you will finally start to make your health a priority. Up until this defining moment, you have probably put your career and other people ahead of you. But now, you are number one! Honestly, you can't give to others what you don't have yourself. You can't respect, admire, or even love others unless you already have these qualities.

I always laugh when I hear about young people who have poor self-esteem, but fall madly "in love" with each other. It's like two bank-rupt people thinking that the other person will bail them out of their financial pit. I had a marriage counselor once come in and talk to my health class about relationships and marriage. She asked the question: "What's the most important thing you can bring into a relationship?" My students were answering things like, money, power, property, a good body, and other traits that they thought would be desirable. The coun-selor smiled and shook her head, and then told them that they were all wrong. "The most important thing is self-esteem. You have to love your-self before you can love anyone else." Trust me. That made an impres-sion! So remember that you will always be the captain of your team and will be making the important decisions during the game.

The next level is comprised of your teammates, usually your friends, family, colleagues and people who share your common interests. Take a look at the people in your life now that would be your teammates in the aging game. Do you need to recruit some new teammates? I remem-ber that's what my first successful coach did when he started building a team that became a national championship team. At first, we were pa-thetic——we let the other teams beat up on us. Some quit because they didn't like losing or training that hard, and a few others, like me, stayed because we loved the game and our coach was a genius. As we started getting new players to come to our team who were serious about train-ing and committing to the sport, we started to move through the ranks, and eventually won the National Title. The team we started with would have never achieved that goal. Also, our team was so fun! We would do anything for each other and always had each other's back.

So who is now currently on your team? Do these people in your life support your goals? Do they have the same goals as you do in the sport of aging? Are they ready to take control of their lifestyle to enjoy their life at any age? Or are they the ones that complain about every ache and pain and always say how aging sucks and are looking for others who will listen and empathize with their complaints? I don't know about you, but I can't stand to be around these people. They are the lobsters trying to pull you back into the pot of boiling water. I'm sure you've heard the phrase "Misery loves company." The aging game does not allow complaining. It is about developing your empowerment muscles to take charge. No one can do it alone, so where do you find these teammates? Good question!

Remember the lobster trying to crawl out of the boiling pot? We need people who are crawling out with us or some who are already out of the pot helping us out. The first place to start is with the people who are already in your life who you care about. Your spouse or life partner if you have one, can be a supportive force, or sabotage your efforts. It's imperative that you communicate your desires with this person and if possible, get them to have the same goals. It's hard when one person is making healthy changes and really trying to work towards an optimal life, and his or her partner doesn't want to put in the effort and might even become a negative influence. I'm not saying that this is a reason to leave your partner, but it is a reason to make sure you have a lot of team-mates who are more supportive. The same thing goes for other mem-bers of your family. Some of these people will be active players on your team, and others will be spectators who will hopefully be cheering you on. They might not want to play the game, but most of time they want to watch. Remember that you really can't change others, but then again, you should never let them change you.

Okay, so besides family, the next area is your friends. These can be some of the best teammates, because friends care about each other and are there for each other in times of need. They also usually accept you for who you are and don't try to change you. Good friends like this are golden, and these relationships need to be nurtured. So make sure you let these friends know that you are fired up to take charge of your life and health and tell them how you are doing it. Many times, you will inspire them to do the same. Don't wait for the phone to ring. You need to take the initiative and call or text your friends and see if you can spend some time with them.

So, just like my early volleyball team, that wasn't very good at the game, how do we bring in new teammates to elevate our game? We have to go out and recruit, and the first place is to start in our community. There are many community centers, Senior clubs and YMCA's that have activities for seniors including, exercise classes, games, and dances. There are even some that organize travel excursions and cruises. I remember once on an Alaskan cruise, there was a vivacious group of seniors who literally "rocked the boat" with energy and fun. They made all the young couples and groups seem old. In fact, one man, who was probably in his early forties asked how old he had to be to get into the group. It was almost as if he was jealous!

Also, check with your local recreation departments where they not only offer exercise classes, but also various sports teams. Remember, you are the one who is looking for people you want on your team. If you love singing and music, check with your church and join the choir. If you love books, join a book club, or if you love to write, a writing group, if you love to walk, there are even walking groups you can join. You get the idea. The list is endless, and all you have to do is research these interests in your area, find a group, get over your fear of the unknown, and get out and meet these people. You can also volunteer your services for a needy cause, go back to school, or learn a new trade.

The Internet is also a great resource to get team members. You might not ever meet these people in person, but sometimes they can become your greatest advocates. Online healthy aging communities are now popping up all over the Internet where healthy seniors share tips, stories and support. One of my favorites is www.healthyaging.net. There is also a great resource for mature companionship for people over 50 called Stitch. Their mantra is "everyone needs company regardless of age". The cool thing is that age isn't even a factor. In fact, it's intentionally left off the profiles unless someone wants to include it. You can check it out at: www.stitch.net. People use the site to find friends with the same interests while others use it to find a partner. However, make sure you never share any financial information on dating websites. Unfortunately, there are some unethical people who are not interested in finding company or a relationship. They are looking for money.

There are also two resources that I highly recommend for women. The first one is www.sixtyandme.com , a website founded by Margaret Manning with a community of 150,000 women over 60. Her mission is to help other women her age to live happy, healthy and financially secure lives. The resources and articles are excellent and every woman over 60 should have it bookmarked.

Another excellent resource is a book new book written by Bernice Bratter and Helen Dennis, *Project Renewment; the First Retirement Model for Women.* This book offers a new kind of retirement...one that emphasizes positive change, adventure and enlightenment. Sounds like fun, huh? For more information on the book and how to form a project renewment group, go to www.projectrenewment.com

Facebook is another social media site that I use mostly to stay in touch with friends that no longer live close. It was great to recently connect with several of my high school friends that I hadn't seen or heard from in years. You can also use Skype to keep in touch with family members and friends. So there really isn't any reason to feel that you are alone anymore. And remember, there is no limit to the amount of members you can have on your team.

Another source to find teammates is at your place of work. Who besides you has the same health goals? Spend more time with them, and even plan some activities outside of work. For people who have retired, or don't have a job and are bored, how about checking out an encore career? This is defined as work in the second half of life that combines continued income, greater personal meaning and social impact.

One of my author colleagues worked in corporate America for over thirty years, and then decided to try something totally different.

He wanted to chronicle the lives of the Baby Boomer Population and spent over a year interviewing people from all over the country to see where they were now in their lives. He now has a best- selling book, *In Search of the Baby Boomers,* is having the time of his life, and has more friends and colleagues than ever! If you need help in deciding what encore career might be good for you check out www.encore.org.

Your medical doctors and practitioners are also members of your team and you should be able to choose them if possible. Besides being excellent at their jobs, they also need to be someone you can talk to about your concerns and answer your questions. Remember that doctors often have huge loads, and cannot spend a lot of time with each patient, so be sure you make the most of the time you have at your appointments. Also, make sure they are aware of any supplements or drugs that you are taking now, because if they do write you a prescription, they need that information so there won't be a dangerous reaction. Most people have not one, but many doctors, such as an internist, gynecologist, ENT, dermatologist, hematologist, chiropractor, and many other specialties. Make sure they are all on the same team and don't conflict with each other. I always like a doctor who utilizes an integrative approach, and encourages you to seek out other doctors and practitioners to go along with their treatments. I know it sounds crazy, but I consider my massage therapist as a member of my team. She knows exactly how to relax my tight muscles and I can talk to her about anything since the massages last at least an hour.

I wish I could say that Health Insurance Companies are a part of your team, but they are more like the officials. They make the decisions as to what they will cover, and what they will not. It's a necessary part of the game when you consider that a one-day stay in most hospitals can cost up to 30,000 dollars. As an athlete and coach for many years, I can tell you that officials are never the same. I had some good, some bad, and some down-right ugly. Obviously, there are many choices in this area and everybody is different in terms of what they can pay and what they want covered. Medicare is for individuals over 65 who have paid into Social Security or are married to someone who has paid their required quarters. It covers 80% and is a godsend for many people who otherwise wouldn't be able to afford insurance as they age.

One last great resource for seniors is AARP. I remember when I turned 50 and got their first letter for me to join. I wasn't retired, so why did they send me information? And how did they know my age? But, I can tell you, it is a great resource and I do encourage you to check it out. I once did a book signing at their convention in Atlanta, and I was shocked to see so many seniors so actively engaged and happy. Their list of resources and support is incredible and they are very helpful and knowledgeable in answering any questions regarding health issues, financial planning, retirement, long term care, and many other concerns. Make sure AARP is on your team!

In summary, remember that we cannot play this game by ourselves. It would be like me setting a volleyball against a wall and keeping score. What fun is in that? Also, alone we can be beaten easily, whereas there is strength in numbers. If I put one rubber band between your hands, you could probably break it easily. But if I gave you 10 or more and wrapped them around your hands, it would be very hard, if not impossible to break them. So don't be in survival mode. Let's be in a thriving mode and have an awesome team to play the aging game.

CHAPTER NINE

AGEISM AND SCAMS

"If you don't have enough pride, you're going to get your butt beat every play."

—*Gale Sayers*

THE PHONE RANG WHILE I WAS WRITING, SO I DID WHAT MOST PEOPLE would do. I let the phone take a message. When I went back to listen I was shocked by hearing a man speak urgently in broken English. He said that he was from the IRS and that I was in trouble and would need to call back within 24 hours or I would be arrested.

What the??? I played it again just to make sure my hearing wasn't failing me, and then realized that I had heard it right. I knew right off that it was a scam because my husband and I have faithfully paid our taxes on time for over 40 years. How could we be in trouble with the IRS? I wrote down the phone number and called our local better business bureau. When I reported the incident, the man asked me if I called the number. I said of course not, and he said that was the right thing to do. I gave him the number and asked if there was any way that they could stop these people. I imagine that if someone did have a problem with their taxes, that he or she would call the number and do what they were told.

He said that they couldn't do anything because these people are pros, and they feed on the weak and are hard to catch because they move around. "But I have their number!" The man from the better business bureau just laughed and said that they change the numbers all the time. Then I asked what he meant about "feeding on the weak." He said that the aging population is a huge target for scammers because they are perceived as trusting and not familiar with today's technology. So we are the weak huh? *I don't think so.*

Psychologists and neuroscientists are identifying strategies that individuals can use to improve their mind-sets about aging with benefits for their health and well-being. In a recent study, for example, researchers at institutions including the Yale School of Public Health found that older individuals who were subliminally exposed to positive messages about aging showed long-term improvements in self-image, strength, and balance and tended to live 7.5 years longer than those with negative stereotypes. What counted for this finding is that people with positive age stereotypes have a stronger will to live, and that this might affect their ability to adapt to the challenges of aging. According to Becca Levy, who led the Yale study: "Negative stereotypes about aging are a public-health issue. What people aren't aware of is that they have the ability to overcome and resist negative stereotypes, and compensate for the ill effects of automatic ageism." [1]

That, my fellow teammates, is one of our goals. Besides being as healthy and lively as possible as we age, we have to turn around the current paradigm about aging, and we can only do this by our example and leadership. We must speak up when we hear inaccurate assumptions about aging. As competitors in the Sport of Aging, not only are we on a mission to achieve optimal living as we age, but we must also be ambassadors and educate and motivate others. Ageism is age discrimination, and as we know there have been several groups who have experienced discrimination, including Blacks, Women, the Disabled, and Overweight People. However, these groups have champions who have helped in changing the tide and perceptions about these groups. Where are our Age Champions? Who will speak out and change our current attitudes and the unfair negative age stereotypes that permeate our society? I think it starts with us! We need to have more role models of people who will reset the image of Aging in America. I have a couple of great examples of people who I consider to be part of my team. Their stories are at the end of the chapter. These people are on a mission to not grow old, no matter how long they live!

According to Laura Robbins from the American Society of Aging, "If you are not already part of a group disadvantaged by prejudice, just wait a couple of decades—you will be. Unlike all other prejudices, ageism is relevant to every person fortunate enough to make it beyond a sixth decade of life. Unlike the attention focused on other prejudices, however, ageism has been poorly studied and rarely confronted. Until recently, little was known about its origins and consequences." [2]

So it's time for us to take a look at what's going on, why, and how we can correct it. If you are a baby boomer like me, born between 1946 and 1964, you know that our generation is known for being non-traditional and breaking through glass ceilings. So we are the ones who can make our final impact as a generation, and change how our society views aging.

How does ageism affect our lives? Healthcare is one area with people either being untreated or over-treated. My husband once experienced this when he went to see a specialist and the doctor had the nerve to say that he didn't treat older people. My husband is in excellent shape and could have run circles around this jerk of a doctor, and he won't treat my husband because of his age? Also, ageism limits our abilities to be hired or promoted and many people experience harassment on the job because of their age. I know one woman who was at the top of her company until a young boss was hired who took an instant dislike to her because he felt threatened by her experience. He started to micromanage her and criticized everything she did while letting the younger employees get away with massive mistakes. She would just look at him like he was a confused 8 year old, which was how old he was when she was hired at the company. I wish I could report that things got better, but so far she still is struggling and will at some point decide if it's worth staying.

And this discrimination doesn't just happen in healthcare or at work. Many older adults complain that they had been insulted or mistreated because of their age. What's even worse, sometimes, is being ignored. I remember walking into a store a while back to get a gift for my daughter, and it was almost impossible to get someone to wait on me. I know I didn't fit the demographic that was so visible in the store at the time, but I had money and was going to spend a lot to get her a great gift. It was their loss.

So how can we change this untrue, damaging paradigm of aging that older people are a burden on society and are deserving of these attitudes? First, we must get involved in society and continue to make a difference and help and inspire others. We have to quit complaining about our age or age related symptoms, and focus on the good in our lives. We need to aspire to be the best versions of ourselves, and continue to make positive changes that will give us our best chance to be vital. We need to take charge of our health, clean up our diet, exercise, and realize that we are role models.

Very simply, we cannot give up and let negative attitudes rob us from living a fulfilled life at any age. We need to keep our sense of humor and not get thrown off when age throws us a curve. We can be amazing examples to the next generation as to what 60, 70, 80, 90 and even above 100 years looks like. We can do this; I know we can. We just need to put on our helmets and get into the game instead of being on the bench or in the stands.

Now about the scams...everyone is a target for scammers, but the older population is more vulnerable because we are perceived as being too trusting, not experienced with computers, and enticed by bargains. Also, people with mild cognition problems can be a huge target. And these scammers are everywhere: on the phone, in the mail, online and sometimes even at your door. This morning, when I opened up my email there was one with the subject line: "Awful Trip Please Help!" It was supposedly from a person who had upholstered our couch, but I knew it couldn't be from him: Here's what it said: (the typos are a part of the email)

"Good Morning. I hope you get this on time!!! Sorry to disturb you but I had to send this message to you due to an unforeseen circumstance I encountered. I traveled to Manila for a short vacation but unfortunately for me, I had an accident of which I dislocated my arm and my head got bruised. The driver of the cab passed on due to internal bleeding and injuries he sustained on his head. I have not been able to reach any one due to the fact that my cell phone, credit cards and some valuable document were all missing after the accident.

Thanks goodness am safe but presently in the hospital due to injuries I sustained. I am only in public library to reach out for help through this medium since it the only way out. Please kindly get back to me as you receive this message so that I can tell you how to help me out I depend on you. Thanks, Eli"

First of all, I know that Eli does not speak like this and can surely spell better since he is a businessman. Obviously I'm not going to respond to the email, but I will call his number on his business card and let him know that he was hacked and that the hackers are using his name to scam his contacts. The same thing happened to me three years ago when I couldn't get into my email account. My nephew came to dinner and said that he thought I was in Ethiopia since I emailed him and asked for money. He was laughing because he knew that I had been hacked. I guess this scam is still alive and well and the scammers will keep doing it as long as someone believes it is real.

I already mentioned the IRS scam, which is so irritating because the caller is so forceful and aggressive. I'm sure they are scaring some people who really might be in trouble with the IRS. But if you ever get one of these calls, just ignore it. If you were in trouble with the IRS, they would send you something in the mail. And even then, I would have that checked out.

The one scam that is probably the biggest one right now is the Tech Support Scam. It works in two ways. First, you get an unsolicited call from someone claiming to be with Microsoft or Windows tech support who say viruses have been detected on your computer. You are told to go to a certain web site and follow its instructions. Or, your computer may start to malfunction and a screen comes up saying that you have a virus and to call this number to fix it. If you get a call, hang up and call a reliable person. I personally like the Geek Squad and have been with them for over a year. Remember, don't click any links in an unsolicited email from Microsoft or pop up ads promising to speed up your computer. That's probably how the computer gets the virus.

Another common scam is called the Silent Call. You pick up the phone, say hello, and there's no one on the line. How annoying! However, it is for a reason. It's called a robocall, and automated computer system making tens of thousands of calls to build a list of humans to target for theft. My husband loves to answer the phone, and I keep telling him to stop and check the caller ID first. Remember, don't answer the phone if the number is unfamiliar or it says "unknown name."

And then there are the lotteries! You get an email or a phone call that says that you have won millions of dollars! Wow! Except then you realize that you didn't enter any contest, and are told that you have to give them a certain amount of money to get the prize....hello! That is illegal. If you do give them money, you'll never hear from them again, and they can't be traced. Also, be aware gift vouchers. If you get an unsolicited email from a company like McDonalds or Subway or Carl's Junior, or any company and it offers a free gift card, but you must activate a link to activate it, don't click it! It's probably a phishing scam where they install malware or viruses on your computer or try to gather personal information.

Finally, the cruelest is called the Grandparent Scheme where someone calls and says that he or she is your grandchild and needs money, or even worse, that he or she was kidnapped and you need to send a ransom. These scammers even try to find voices that sound realistic. Here's another reason to make sure you are in contact with your family so you won't be tricked.

Supplements are another area of concern, because manufacturers and distributors do not need FDA approval to sell their dietary supplements. As a result, the people marketing the supplements can make all sorts of extreme false claims. They use a technique called copywriting, or should I say persuasive writing to tap into people's emotions to get them to buy products. I took some courses in copywriting, and I can tell you, the great copywriters will get people to buy almost anything. Weight loss and anti-aging supplements make huge amounts of money, lots of promises, but most of the time don't produce any results and can be dangerous. I have tried many supplements over the years, and I can tell you from my experience that most of them do not work; as far as losing weight goes, the only thing you will lose is money. Here are some sure fire ways to spot a supplement scam.

Promises super-fast weight loss. For example: "Lose 30 pounds in 30 days!

Everybody will lose weight, 100% success rate.

Lose weight permanently, never diet again.

Eat anything you want and how much you want and still lose weight.

You don't need to exercise!"

Testimonials, especially from celebrities. (These may or may not be authentic.)

Uses terms such as "scientific breakthrough," "miracle pill," "secret formula" to describe their product.

Has before and after pictures, most of which have been altered by computer retouching.

Isn't sold in the stores.

Claims to remove fat from certain areas of your body, like your waist.

Lacks scientific evidence to support claims, or makes up bogus science to support claims.

The bottom line is always "if it sounds too good to be true, it probably is."

These are just a few of the scams that are out there. Others are charity scams, online dating scams, and medical identity theft among others. A great resource is www.scambusters.org, an online publication on internet fraud. I actually signed up to get their weekly issue and if you are concerned about being scammed, I would suggest you do the same. (It's free) Also, AARP has several article about scams that target seniors. Let's stand up to these scammers and show that we are not the weak!

Here are two stories of great role models who are taking on Aging as a Sport and standing up to ageism. The first is a fiery woman, Connie Rayna who turned her life around at fifty years of age, and Nick Prestia, my media advisor who has incredible energy, joy and bubbles with enthusiasm. I don't see either of them ever getting "old." We need to have more people like Connie and Nick in our lives and in the media. Here are their stories:

CONNIE RAYNA

"Hi there, Coach Connie here and I'm living life to the fullest. At the age of 52 I tried out for the USA National Canoe and Kayak Olympic Team and made the cut. Now in my late 50's, I'm in the best shape of my life and probably more fit, healthy and active than most 20 year olds. I embrace this quote from George Burns: 'Young, Old. Just Words.'

I haven't always been this way. When I turned 50 I felt miserable. I was overweight, lacked energy, had brain fog, was swollen and most times unable to do anything physical without getting out of breath. I led a fast paced life in technology and was on the road traveling every week. Add to this the age factor and the new body adjustments and RED LIGHTS should have been flashing 'WARNING, DISASTER AHEAD!'

Everyone has a low point...you know, that point you reach when you 'hit the wall.' I'll never forget the day I boarded a flight from LA to San Francisco and realized I no longer fit in the plane seat without spilling over into my neighbor's space. The person next to me looked disgusted and I remember everyone around me giving me 'the stare.' I had already felt bad about myself and now I felt like my secret was out. This was the worse day of my life and the best thing that ever happened. It was this day I realized things needed to change.

I was never one to do things in a 'quiet way.' In fact, I'm probably a Type AA personality if one even exists. I began my journey of transformation and signed up to trek the Himalaya Mountains in Bhutan. I decided if I was going to make a change, I needed a purpose, something pretty big, and something that would scare me into getting serious about getting fit. I joined a gym and hired a health coach who taught me about food and a new way to eat without dieting. She changed my life and over the course of a year and a half, I lost 65 inches, completed the trek in Bhutan and got in the best shape of my life.

This change sparked a desire in me to learn more about nutrition, so I went back to school, resigned from my corporate job and today help others get back on track to live a full life of health and happiness. It's incredible as I feel my life has just started and I'm living my dream!"

—*Connie Rayna CHHC, PMP*

www.Xtreme_Measures.com

NICK PRESTIA

"I was born in 1949. While growing up in the 50's & 60's I was very competitive & into various sports. I excelled at baseball & football. I also played basketball along with Hockey / Ice Skating, roller skating & Bowling. At that time soccer was not a sport. Occasionally in gym we would line up on two sides of the gym, the same as dodgeball. On the days we kicked the ball instead of throwing it, they called it soccer!

When I went to High School in the 60's I was into football & track. Fitness training, which at that time was being pioneered in some small circles, was not known outside of those circles. Our football coach told us to stay away from the weight room! He said it was for body build-ers not athletes. The theory then was that if you bulked-up, like a body builder, you would lose speed & agility.

However, we did have 2 special rules for all football players that ap-plied during the football season. Number One was, everyone had to get a buzz-cut. Number Two was no cigarette smoking allowed, except for coach!

Being aggressive and competitive I was in a hurry to accomplish things. So I got married three months before the age of 19! Once married it was work and family first. Sports became hobbies that you did once a week or so. Combining less physical activity with a lot more eating was another bad choice. I thought it's my food, eat all you wish! While being that young, gaining ten to fifteen pounds per year was not something that I noticed. Also, moderate weight gains after marriage along with aging were considered normal by many people at that time.

After continuing on this path for nine years I finally noticed that I had gained over one-hundred pounds! A friend of mine who found himself in a similar predicament some years earlier recommended that I try 'The Air Force Diet.' He looked incredible. I thought he was always thin so I tried it. This diet was the original Atkin's low carb diet. It wasn't the healthier version that's now used. I liked the idea of being able to eat a large amount of food while losing weight. I liked the idea of not feeling hungry. It was meat and fats are okay, but no more than 30 grams a day of carbohydrates / sugars.

After ten months I had lost 115 pounds and was back to my High School weight. At this time, I was smoking between two and three packs of cigarettes a day. Because of smoking, after one hour of racquetball I would be gasping for air. I had to stop and catch my breath if there were more than three flights of stairs. I could run around the bases, but not much farther. I had tried to quit several times unsuccessfully. A friend of mine who also was very competitive was badgering me daily at work because he quit smoking. He bet me one-hundred dollars that I couldn't quit smoking for one month. Thanks to my competitive nature, I won the bet and have not smoked since. The cravings remained for several years but I resisted.

ALMOST 30 YEARS LATER

After a car accident at the age of fifty-six I required physical therapy for my neck, shoulders, and back. My cardio fitness level was still high because of activity sports like hiking. But my muscles were all getting mushy. In therapy I was told that when you have an accident, your weaknesses are exposed. They said that strengthening the muscles around my neck, back and shoulders could protect me from some potential future injuries. I took advantage of a special offer to join Lifetime Fitness Club via the Therapy office based on their recommendations.

After two years of working out I was back to my high-school weight. My waist was three inches smaller, and I had guns I could show off to my grandkids! In addition, I always have annual physicals and blood work. My cardio is so good that my blood pressure is always in the low end of normal. The nurses taking it are always impressed. My blood sugar was normal and my cholesterol while at the high end of normal, has twice the minimum number of good cholesterol required. To summarize, at 59 I was in the best shape of my life.

LIFE CHANGES

Then at the age of 59 I had a heart attack! Not only did I not know this, but I didn't believe the doctor when he told me that I had a heart attack. I didn't have the classic symptoms. There was no elephant standing on my chest, nor arm pain. I witnessed my dad having these symptoms and even drove him to the hospital so I thought I knew what a heart attack looked like. While my kids and grandkids were visiting one Sunday I had to excuse myself and go to my room because of extreme shoulder pain. I had pain like this before from working out too hard. The difference this day was I could not find any position that would ease the pain and the pain level was extremely high. It subsided after several hours.

The next day I did my early morning workout without any unusual pain and went to my office. Because the incident was so unusual I called my doctor. He told me that he was not available and that it would be a good idea to go to immediate-care to be checked. I asked him if he'd be in the next day and convinced him that I was okay and would see him tomorrow afternoon.

When I went to the doctor's office, his nurse came in and said the doctor wanted her to do an EKG before he came in. Her bedside manner was a little lacking. While doing the test and looking at the strip, she said, 'Oh my!' I asked her what was the matter and she said, 'the doctor will be right in.'

The doctor came in and told me that I had had a heart attack, and that an ambulance was on the way! I laughed at him and said, 'no way, I'm in the best shape of my life, test me again!' He said the test would be the same and to relax, the ambulance will be here soon. I told him that I needed to get something from my car, and then they took away my keys so that I couldn't leave! In the ambulance I was calling people telling them about the big mistake the doctor made and laughing about it.

I WAS WRONG. In the emergency room I learned that I had a 100% blockage in one of the hearts main arteries. Fortunately, not the one known as, 'The Widow Maker.' They did angioplasty to clear it and put in a single stint to keep it open. As I mentioned, my father had heart problems and so did my brother. They both had their first heart attacks around the age of 40. They both had multiple by-pass surgery, multiple times. I told the doctor that I thought I had escaped those bad genes because I was 59 years old and never had any health issues. He told me keeping in good shape delayed my genes from catching up with me. But now they did.

Here's the good news. 90 days later I had an echo-cardio stress test. I not only passed with flying colors, but there were no signs of heart-wall damage. The doctor said I had a large number of collateral arteries which had grown across my blockage thus creating a natural bypass. He said this happens to people who are fit and do hard cardio workouts. So things could have been much worse.

How I 'Take On Aging as A Sport'

Nine and a half years later at the age of 66 I'm stronger than ever and am within 3 pounds of my high-school weight. All of my 6 month doctors' visits have been positive. The same goes for my annual physicals. I tell everyone that I feel like a healthy 50-year-old!

Being competitive and type A never completely goes away. My challenge now is to see if I can maintain a health fitness age 10 to 15 years less than my chronological age. In order to do that I've added some new things to my workouts. This makes working out more fun, and also more effective. Last year I've added an 11 station TRX, Cable Machine, and balance ball whole body workout. Last year I started doing an hour plus session of Yoga once a week. This year I am doing Yoga 3 times a week!

When I started Yoga I was interested in increasing my flexibility. Little did I know how much strength is involved in Yoga. For example, I was able to do a right side plank the first time I tried, then when we were supposed to do a left side plank, I fell on my side! All of the balance poses really work your legs and feet. I guess I've become addicted to Yoga! I always feel better after a session than I did at the start.

I eat healthier than I used to, but could always improve in this area. My main objective is to keep moving. The only time I ever feel close to my age is after long periods of inactivity. So I try to keep these periods to a minimum. That's why some fitness trackers tell you when you've been sitting too long and remind you to get up and do a little stretching. Have fun, keep moving as long as you can, and always remember to, 'Take On Aging as A Sport.'"

—*Nick Prestia*

Saint Charles, Illinois

CHAPTER TEN

TAKE GOOD CARE OF YOUR BRAIN

*"The wonderful part of being human is that our computer-like
brain allows, indeed insists, that we continue to learn to the
end of our lives."*

—Ray J. Groves

EVERY ATHLETE AND COACH KNOWS HOW IMPORTANT MENTAL
preparation is when competing in a sport. It's not enough to have
the skills and physical conditioning. The brain has to be focused, flexible
and ready to make adjustments. Sure, there have been many gifted
athletes with amazing physical attributes, but if their minds and brains
are not also trained, these athletes will not be able to perform to their
potential. So as we embark upon taking on aging as a sport, we need to
not only get our bodies into shape, but we also need to get our brains
and minds on board. This is one of the biggest challenges we face as we
age. It's not enough to have a fit body if the brain is not able to do its job.

One of my students once asked me what the difference was between
the brain and the mind. As I struggled to think of the right answer, I noticed he was holding his laptop and suddenly it came to me—an analogy!
I told him that the brain was like the hard drive in his computer, and
the mind was the software. Without the hardware, the software couldn't
function, and without the software, there would be little for the computer to do. My student smiled, and said thanks.

What's amazing is that we all have this incredible organ between our ears that is better than the most amazing computer in the world and it comes with both the hardware and the software, and is always changing, either for better or for worse. The problem is....it didn't come with an instruction manual.

The current statistics are shocking, scary, sad, and a wake-up call to everyone. According to the Alzheimer's Association (www.alz.org) every 67 seconds, someone in the United States develops Alzheimer's. It is the only disease among the top 10 causes of death in America that currently cannot be prevented, cured or even slowed. The future looks scary--- by 2025 the number of people age 65 and older with Alzheimer's disease is estimated to reach 7.1 million, a 40 percent increase from the 5.1 million age 65 and older affected in 2015. [1]

Unfortunately, some of these people will have been some of the best athletes from the past. I know some of these people, and it doesn't make sense to me. Obviously, we have a challenge on our hands. How can this disease be prevented? Will we ever have a cure? How can we take good care of our brains?

Recent research is starting to look promising and offers hope in keeping the brain healthy as we age. Dr. Gary Small, the director of the UCLA Longevity Center and co- author *of 2 Weeks to a Younger Brain* says:

"After three decades of helping thousands of patients improve their memory and mental acuity, I am convinced that our daily lifestyle habits are directly linked to our brain health." [2] His six-lifestyle habits to keep the brain sharp are:

Stay physically active

Stimulate the brain through games, puzzles and education

Manage stress

Maintain good nutrition

Stay socially connected

Keep up with necessary health care

Scientists are now also starting to see a very real correlation between diet and brain health, with many calling Alzheimer's "Type 3 Diabetes." Dr. Mark Hyman believes that the underlying cause is too much sugar on the brain. He says that when we over-consume sugar and don't get enough fat, this leads to what he calls "diabesity" which then leads to inflammation that wreaks havoc on the brain. [3]

We are also learning more about brain functioning, how the mind works, and the capability of the brain to form new connections (neuro-plasticity.) Also, it is now believed by many experts that the brain is capable of regenerating new brain cells. This is exciting because it has long been accepted that the nerve cells in the brain start dying off as we age and that an aging brain and Alzheimer's in our later years are inevitable.

According to the new research pioneered by neuroscientist Dr. Fred Gage of the Salk Institute, adult brains do indeed create new brain cells.[4] The process is called neurogenesis, and according to some experts, is enhanced or reversed by lifestyle choices. In his amazing book, *The Neurogenesis Diet and Lifestyle; Upgrade Your Brain, Upgrade Your Life*, Dr. Brant Cortright emphasizes that the brain keeps growing new brain cells your entire life and your rate of neurogenesis is tied to the quality of your life.[5]

So I would think that since our quality of life really does depend on the quality of our brains, we would want to do everything possible to keep our brains vital and even enhance the brain as we age. Even though there are factors that put us at risk that we can't control, such as genetics and brain trauma, knowing that our lifestyles do affect brain health empowers us to not take our brains for granted.

Obviously, it would be nice if we could just take a pill to keep our brains healthy, but that's not going to happen. According to Dr. Cortright, enhancing neurogenesis is a lifestyle that is all inclusive involving mind, body, heart and spirit. As you know, it takes time to make changes in your life, and you are probably already doing some things to promote new brain growth, but unfortunately, there are also some things that slow it down.

According to Dr. Cortright : "What we believe to be 'normal aging' is actually an artifact of a neurotoxic lifestyle that slows the brain down much more and much faster than necessary. Usually neurogenesis plateaus in middle age. However, this doesn't need to be the case. Neuroscientists recently discovered that neurogenesis can be increased at all ages through proper stimulation."[5]

Here are some of Dr. Cortright's lifestyle choices or proper stimulations in a nutshell that speed up neurogenesis. You'll probably notice that many of these echo what Dr. Small indicated in his book, *2 Weeks to a Younger Brain*. I think it's exciting when you have different specialists looking at the brain from different perspectives, giving similar lifestyle recommendations.

1. Aerobic exercise; any exercise that gets you breathing hard and fast.

2. Foods that increase neurogenesis—Dr. Cortright's Superstars are blueberries or blueberry extract, Omega 3's, Green Tea and Curcumin. These are easy to add to your diet with foods or extracts.

3. A wide range of mental activities. Learn, write, read, discussion groups, video games, and problem solving. Not just one!

4. Avoid a high calorie diet.

5. Music stimulates neurogenesis if it is enjoyable.

6. Love in all its forms.

7. Practice mindfulness (present moment living).

Another expert on brain health is Dr. Amen, a physician; board certified psychiatrist and ten time New Your Times bestselling author. He is the founder and CEO of the Amen Clinics. Dr. Amen believes that brain health is central to all health and life success. He says, "When your brain works right, you work right; and when your brain is troubled, you are much more likely to have trouble in your life." www.danialamenmd.com

Dr. Amen has studied thousands of living brains using SPECT brain imaging, and has actually reversed brain shrinkage and damage with his patients using lifestyle changes as well. You can see pictures on his website of what a healthy living brain looks like in comparison to an unhealthy one.[6]

You can also take an assessment on his website that asks 42 questions and then gives you your brain type and brain fitness score. I love taking assessments, so I took the test and found out that I am Brain Type 1, and my brain fitness score was average with room for improvement. No problem there! I already know that I'm not perfect, and I am always looking to improve, especially as I get older. The cool thing is that he has all kinds of tools on his website that can help fine tune your brain and keep it healthy according to your brain type, its strengths and weaknesses. I haven't tried the tools yet because there is a cost, but if I drive away with my purse on top of the hood again, I might sign up!

The most common complaint I hear from people who have just retired is that they are bored. I have a neighbor who had been working a stressful job for over 25 years and finally decided that he had saved enough money to retire. I remember seeing him shortly afterward, sitting on his porch with his head down. When I congratulated him on his retirement, he just looked up, shook his head, and said "Now what am I going to do?"

This is a widespread concern because many people's lifestyles and sense of worth are tied to their jobs, and when they are no longer working, they are left in limbo. As one of my colleagues told me, "You can only play so much golf."

There are many people who work into their seventies and beyond, and are perfectly happy because they are good at their jobs, have social interactions, and feel that they are contributing to society plus bringing in income. For others, their jobs are the main source of stress in their lives, and retirement puts them on another path that is more stimulating and enjoyable.

My husband, Pat, has been teaching high school for over 50 years, and still gets up every morning at 5:30 a.m., puts on his suit and tie, and goes off to work. He teaches psychology and history and loves his job! The only hard part is correcting all the papers and putting up with inconsistencies with the administration. He always says that he will retire soon, but I really don't think so. If he does, he'll need to find activities to fill his empty time that are stimulating, new, and productive. Why is this so important?

The answer lies in neuroplasticity, or the ability of our neural circuits in the brain to change or increase their connections in response to new activities. These new connections promote better brain functioning, a sense of well-being, and help keep our brains young. The brain likes to learn new things and be challenged at any age! According to Dr. Giroux, the activities that promote neuroplasticity are activities that are more intense, require us to learn new things, or experience positive and life enriching experiences.[7]

What's cool is that when we get older and no longer have to work, we have time to play with neuroplasticity! It's finally time for the brain to have some fun!

Unfortunately, what happens too often is that as we age we get lazy, and use only our old neural pathways and do the same things over and over. If we really want to win at aging and make the second half of life better than the first, we have to keep learning and always be a student of life. We need to expose ourselves to new activities that are engaging and challenging and require us to learn new techniques and ideas. Stepping out of our comfort zones is fun, exhilarating, and just what the brain craves. We just have to suspend our egos, and not worry about making mistakes or being embarrassed. Seriously, who really cares if we make mistakes anymore?

Albert Einstein once said, "Intellectual growth should commence at birth and cease only at death". So keep learning my friends! Don't just engage in activities in which you excel. Keep the brain active, curious, and engaged! We work out our muscles and our heart, but the most important part of our body is our brain because it is the command center of the entire body. So make sure you are feeding it well, not taking in toxins, and stimulating it with challenges to keep it active. Also, the brain needs to rest as well, so those eight hours of sleep a night are really important!

So always remember to take good care of your brain. Don't take the most important organ in your body for granted.

CHAPTER ELEVEN

STAY IN THE GAME UNTIL THE END

"Youth is not a time of life; it is a state of mind. Nobody grows old by merely living a number of years, but to give up enthusiasm wrinkles the soul."

—*Samuel Ullman*

I T TAKES A COMPETITOR TO WANT TO BE ON THE COURT OR FIELD AT the end when the game is on the line. These people want the ball! They are ready to take the responsibility even if it comes down to a final few seconds and the win or loss depends on them. Trust me; they wouldn't want it any other way. Are you ready to have the ball in your hands when it comes to end of life decisions? I hope so... because no one but you should make these choices. However, because of unforeseen circumstances, other people make these decisions every day, and sometimes they are wrong.

One of the biggest fears senior have is that they will outlive their money resources. I don't think anyone wants to work forever, especially at a job that is not fulfilling, so it's important to have a plan that will work for you.

Brian Weatherdon, one of the top coaches on finance got into the business of helping people plan their financial future because of people he knew who were severely stressed out because at their most vulnerable time of life, they were left high and dry. He tells of an 83 year old woman who died of financial stress and another couple who told him that they had 33 months to live. When he asked why 33 months, they said because that was how long their money would last. When it was gone, so were they.[1]

Obviously if we want to be in the aging game at the end, we need to be able to take care of ourselves financially. It's great to have your health, but if you run out of money, you most certainly won't be happy, and the stress could kill you.

This is an area most people didn't consider when they were younger, especially the boomers. I was one of those people. I lived from paycheck to paycheck and when I got my first credit cards, if we couldn't afford something for the kids or were unable to take a trip, the first thing out of my mouth was "I've got CREDIT!" It's no surprise that after several years I fell into the pit that so many people do who want it all, but can't afford it. It took me over 10 years to get out of debt, and I learned a hard lesson. Now I pay off my credit cards each and every month and if I can't afford something, I won't buy it. I never what to be in that place again.

So what's the best plan to have financial security, especially at the end of the game? The truth is, people are different, so their plan should align with their values and the money should last their whole life. It really is about common sense. Most financial planners will offer what Brian Weatherdon calls the "Flatline Model" of financial planning. In other words, have the same amount of money available every month throughout the life span, let's say from 65 to 95 years. Well, that doesn't make sense because in the first part of your retirement, you probably want to travel and do some fun things to knock off your bucket list. In the middle you might want to back off a little because you went so hard at the beginning, and then the last stage, you probably will need more money for health expenses. You don't want to not be able to get a life-saving treatment just because you can't afford it. That kind of planning would be more realistic and also more aligned with a person's needs.

So, in summary, you don't want to be afraid of money, or should I say, running out of money. Make sure you talk to a financial planner who can design a plan that meets your needs and values. I highly advise you to check out Brian Weatherdon's website, www.GuaranteedIncome4Life.ca Remember that if you want to be your best at the end of the game, you need to "take care of business."

A while back my sister was in a coma, and her outlook for survival was not good. In fact, when I was sleeping in the waiting room one night, I heard two nurses talking about my sister as they walked past me. One of them said that if she did come out of her coma that she would most likely be in a vegetative state the rest of her life. I'll never forget hearing that. Our family had a very difficult discussion as to what we thought her wishes would be. She was on life support at the time, and we were looking at a difficult choice as to whether to disconnect her from life support soon, or keep her on for an extended period of time. I remember hearing what the nurses said and voted that I thought she would want to be disconnected instead of coming back and not be able to communicate, move, or even know where she was. Her husband didn't want her to die, ever, so he chose to keep her on life support for as long as they could. I remember thinking that if I was his wife, that I would not want him to make that choice for me.

However, a miracle happened and she came out of her coma just a few days later, and is now healthier than ever. So, you never know. However, it did stir something deep inside that is still burning. I want to be in the game at the end. Even if I am unable to communicate my choices at the time, I want to have made them known before, and hope my wishes are granted. That is the power of an advanced medical directive. You are still in the game, making the last shot.

So what are medical directives? These are documents designed to outline a person's preferences in regard to medical treatments and interventions should a person become incapacitated and not be able to communicate his or her medical decisions. Examples when these directives would be enforced would be coma, brain injury, persistent vegetative states, strokes, and advanced Alzheimer's disease. There are three categories of advanced directives: two are for medical decisions, and one is for business and financial decisions.

The first directive is called a Living Will that specifies what medical treatments are desired or even more importantly, not desired. They can be very specific or general in nature. Here is one of the most common living will statements: "If I suffer an incurable, irreversible condition or disease and my doctor determines that my condition is terminal, I direct that life sustaining measures that would serve only to prolong my dying be withheld or discontinued." [2]

A more specific one would be: "In the event of an accident or incurable, irreversible disease and my doctors determines that there is no chance for survival, I direct that life sustaining measures that would serve to only prolong my life be withheld or discontinued, except for any pain medication that would help to ease my transition." I would probably go for this one!

Besides a Living Will, everyone should also have a Health Care Proxy, where another person is assigned to make health care decisions if you cannot make them on your own. The health care proxy has the same rights to refuse or request treatment on your behalf. My husband is my Health Care Proxy, because he knows me better than anyone, and I know would not only honor my wishes, but also do what is the best for me.

The last Advanced Directive is the DPOA, or Durable Power of Attorney. This directive puts someone in charge of your finances who can write checks, pay bills, and make bank transactions, income tax filing, or any other business transactions if you are not able to do so. This person needs to be someone you absolutely trust, because I have heard many horror stories of people who take advantage of this directive.

Why are these directives so important? The main reasons are because they honor your autonomy and dignity and also relieve a lot of stress for both your family and physicians when it comes to decision-making. However, the shocking fact is that four out of five American adults do not have advanced medical directives. I guess no one wants to think about dying, but as we all know, we are probably not going to get off this planet alive anytime soon. So, if we want to be in the game at the end, we need to step up and talk to our families and also fill out the documents.

Where do you get the documents? The easiest places are from your doctor's office, attorneys' offices, hospitals and even some post offices. Many hospitals will have you fill them out before you are admitted, which sometimes takes people by surprise. I remember filling them out before I had a minor procedure many years ago. To be honest, it kind of scared me because I thought that maybe they weren't telling me about all the risks of the procedure. But it was standard policy for that hospital, and it sure got me thinking!

Another more recent development is the Right to Die Law. California is the fifth state that has approved this kind of legislation, however more states are expected to follow in the upcoming years. So how does it work? The conditions are very strict and actually very few people will qualify to have this choice. First, two separate doctors must diagnose a life span of less than six months, and a written and two separate oral requests must be submitted by the patient at least fifteen days apart. The decision cannot be made by anyone else, so the health care proxy will not work in this case. The person must also have the mental capacity to make his or her decision so those with dementia or other brain dysfunctions would not qualify. If a person does qualify, then the ending of his or her life occurs with a doctor's assistance.

When it comes to the ethics of the Right To Die Law, there are many people who are in support or strongly opposed. I don't pretend to know what is right or wrong in this case, but even though I don't think I would chose this option, I don't judge anyone who would, as it is their life, and people should have a choice as to how they want to die.

A final way to exert your wishes is to take care of business so your family doesn't have to do this when you are gone. Decisions like burial plots, caskets, or cremation ideally should also be your decision, and it would also really help your family if these were not only planned ahead of time, but also paid for in advance. I know of one woman who wanted to have her ashes put inside a stuffed pink bear and have it showcased on her husband's mantel. One man wanted to be buried in his car. Obviously, these requests are a bit strange, but these people got what they wanted, although the pink bear might not have a long shelf life on the mantel if her husband decides to remarry.

Chapter Twelve

Your Game Plan

"In the end, it's not the years in your life that count. It's the life in your years."

—Abraham Lincoln

THE BEST GAME PLANS ARE ALWAYS SHORT AND SIMPLE TO IMPLEMENT. In the Sport of Aging we want to have a competitive edge in the game of life, especially during the second half. As your coach, I want you to be successful, motivated, and ready for any challenges that come your way as you take on aging as a sport.

Here is a ten point game plan that you can use and tweak whenever necessary. No one is perfect when it comes to lifestyle choices and we will sometimes lose a game here and there, but that is the nature of sports. I don't know any high-level athletes in any sport who have not been beaten more than once at some point in their careers. However, getting beat never made them quit, and neither should you.

After all, this is your life. The challenge is to look upon the second half of your life as an adventure, have no expectations, and be ready for anything!

THE TEN POINT GAME PLAN

1. **Attitude.** No athlete or coach ever enters a game thinking that he or she is going to lose. Even if the odds are against them, they are ready to compete and go for the win. Having a positive attitude when it comes to aging is imperative, not only for us as individuals, but also for society as a whole. Looking for the good instead of what is wrong is a quality that we can all possess. A "Can Do" attitude is deep inside each and every one of us, and needs to be activated as we enter the game. Stop whining about your age. Be proud to have made it this far along the road of life----and know that there's still more to come! Have a curious, open attitude, and enjoy the rest of the ride.

2. **Know your numbers.** As an athlete, you were probably assessed many times by your coaches, and knew your performance numbers, for example: shooting percentages, spiking percentages, aces per game, passing efficiency, and other statistics that determined your proficiency. Knowing these numbers provided a baseline as to how to determine improvement. In the aging game, we also need to know our numbers including blood pressure, resting heart rate, blood sugar, triglycerides, cholesterol, LDL, HDL, body composition, and other tests that show how our body is functioning. Knowing our numbers, keeping them in check, and trying to improve them if they are in unhealthy ranges are personal responsibilities.

3. **Move every day for at least 30 minutes**. You know what happens when you don't move much during the day. You get stiff and sore. When you played your sport, you didn't just exercise on game days. You probably trained each and every day so that you were ready to perform on game days. It's no different in the game of aging. Exercise is not only advised as we age...it is imperative. I'm not just talking about the effects on the muscles and

heart. New research has shown that exercise is also imperative for brain health. So if you are not already doing so, make moving for at least 30 minutes a day a priority. It can be any form of exercise, even walking. Just do it! Moving more than 30 minutes a day is even better!

4. **Eat to fuel your life.** We are all different in terms of our diets and preferences. Now is the time to clean up our diets and start adding more fruits and vegetables, and lightening up on animal proteins and processed foods. I know that habits are hard to break, but realizing the power of food, to either make us sick and fatigued or to energize and fuel our lives is one of the most important things we can do to enjoy our lives to the fullest as we age, and also prevent disease. Try to crowd out the unhealthy processed foods with whole foods. Making small changes in your diet will make a huge difference in your quality of life. Also, avoid sugar like the plague. Sugar does nothing good for your body and can put you at risk for just about every chronic disease. It is the "devil in disguise." Don't be tempted!

5. **Make your health and life your top priority.** If you are like a lot of people, you have probably put others above yourself when it comes to priorities. You take care of your kids, your spouse, friends and family before you even think of taking care of yourself. However, as we enter the landscape of aging, we need to upgrade ourselves to number one. When you think about it, you can't really help anyone until you help yourself and are at your best. The person who will always have your back and be your best advocate is YOU. So stop trying to please everyone else and take a good look at what you want and need. Then make the time available to take care of you.

6. **Learn or experience something new each and every day.** This isn't just for fun. It's for brain health! In order to keep our brains healthy, we need to stimulate them each and every day in order

to make new neural connections and keep the ones we have. Our brain is the most important organ in our body. We need to exercise it just like we exercise our muscles and our hearts. Remember that there is always something new to learn or experience; no one has done it all or knows it all. So get creative!

7. **Reach out to others**. One of the most common complaints of older people is that they are lonely. However, we can't wait for the phone to ring or for people to come to us. Everybody is busy, or supposedly they are. So if we want to have social stimulation, we need to reach out to others. Call your friends and family members and see how they are doing. Join groups in your community that share your interests. Volunteer your services or mentor kids or people who are just starting out in their careers. Be around children, who most of the time will light up your life and make you see the world through new eyes. Just remember that if you are lonely, you don't have to be. But it does take initiative on your part to have people in your life who are supportive and fun!

8. **Laugh a lot.** Laughter really can be the best medicine. There are many studies that indicate actual chemical changes occur in the body while you are laughing—like secreting dopamine in the brain—the feel good chemical. So find opportunities to laugh, especially at yourself. Too often we take life, the world, and all the problems and challenges too seriously. I love going to our local Comedy Club after dealing with students all day. There's nothing like listening to a good comic after a hard day at school that can get you to see life's absurdities in a new light and make you laugh.

9. **Live your purpose and passion**. In the second half of life, many of us have the opportunity to get an encore career, where we finally have an opportunity to follow our passion and purpose. Being "on purpose" and "following your passion" is more important now than ever. We finally have a chance to get it right and enjoy and use our talents before we make our final exit.

10. **Never, ever, give up on you**. I see this too often. People use this excuse all the time: "I'm too old to _____". *You're not too old to do anything that you really want to do*. Where there's a will and a desire, there's a way. So, never, ever give up on your life. Each and every day is an opportunity to share, experience life, and make a difference. As my dad always says: "Refuse to get old no matter how long you live!"

So there you have it.... a game plan that works for people like you and me who want to enjoy their lives all the way to the end. My friend and former volleyball teammate, Patty Bright, said it best on her deathbed when she told her husband, "What a wild, fun ride!"

I wish you the best wild ride possible full of love, joy and fulfillment to the end. I want you to be one of those people who is not afraid of death because you have lived your life to the fullest, gave your best effort, and have faith in what's up next.

I want to leave you with two of my favorite quotes about death. After reading them, I realize that I'm not ready to graduate yet. I still have some courses to take, but when I do make my final exit, I have nothing to fear.

"I've told my children that when I die, to release balloons in the sky to celebrate that I graduated. For me, death is a graduation."—Elisabeth Kubler-Ross, physician.

Finally, the last words of Steve Jobs: "Oh wow! Oh wow! Oh wow!"

It will be interesting to discover what that was all about!

ABOUT THE AUTHOR

SHARKIE ZARTMAN IS A FORMER ALL-AMERICAN VOLLEYBALL ATHLETE and champion competitor at UCLA where her jersey was retired. She was a member of the U.S. Women's National Volleyball Team and also competed in the Women's Professional Volleyball Association for five years and is a member of the California Beach Volleyball Hall of Fame.

As a coach, Sharkie led El Camino College to nine league and two state titles, and with her husband, Pat, she helped the South Bay Spoilers win multiple national titles.

Sharkie holds degrees in kinesiology and instructional technology. She teaches health and fitness at the community college level and hosts "Sharkie's Pep Talk" on Healthy Life Radio where she motivates people to take charge of their health and wellness. Sharkie is a certified Health Coach with the official sanction of the New York State Education Department and the Institute of Integrative Nutrition.

Sharkie has authored five books, including:

Shark Sense, Getting in Touch With Your Inner Shark

So You Think You Can Coach Kids?

Youth Volleyball; The Guide for Coaches and Parents

Yoga For Health And Fitness

There's A Place

Her passion has always been to bring out the best in her students, athletes, readers and listeners. She has two daughters and lives in Hermosa Beach, California with her husband of forty years, Pat.

Resources

Introduction

1. Mandy Oaklander, "Your Attitude about Aging May Impact How You Age" TIME; Dec 7, 2015, http//www. Time.com/4138476/ aging_alzheimers_ disease.

Chapter One

1. Roger Landry, *Live Long, Die Short A Guide to Authentic Health and Successful Aging*. (Austin, Greenleaf Book Group Press,2014.)
2. Donald J Hurzeler, *Designated For Success*. (Malvern, CPCU Society, 2004)

Chapter Two

1. Heart Disease Risk Factor Index: www.diseaseriskindex.harvard.edu
2. The American Cancer Society: www.cancer.org

Chapter Three

1. Bruce Lipton, *Biology of Belief; Unleashing the Power of Consciousness, Matter and Miracles* (Carlsbad, Hay House, 2005)
2. Robert Sapolsky, *Why Zebras don't Get Ulcers* (New York, Holt, 1994)

CHAPTER FOUR

1. Roger J. Williams, *Biochemical Individuality: The Basis for the Genetotrophic Concept* (Texas, University of Texas Press, 1970)

CHAPTER FIVE

1. Fredrick Hahn, Michael R. Eades, and Mary Dan Eades, *The Slow Burn Fitness Revolution; The Slow Motion Exercise That Will Change Your Body in 30 Minutes a Week.* (New York, Broadway Books, 2005)

CHAPTER SIX

1. "EWG's 2015 Shopping Guide to Pesticides in Produce" Retrieved March 19, 2016 , www.ewg.org/foodnews
2. Stacy Simon "World Health Organization: Processed Meats Cause Cancer" October 26, 2015, www.cancer.org

CHAPTER SEVEN

1. Deepak Chopra. "Primordial Sound Meditation" www.chopra.com
2. Dr. Herbert Benson. The Relaxation Response, (New York, Harper Collins Publishers,, Inc. 1975)
3. Morone "Mindfulness Meditation for the Treatment of Chronic Low Back Pain" Retrieved February 26, 2010, www.pubmed.gov
4. Brian Seaward. *Health of the Human Spirit* (Needham Heights, Allyn & Bacon, MA.)
5. Catherine Ann Jones, *Heal Your Self with Writing,* (Studio City, Divine Arts, 2013)

CHAPTER EIGHT

Recommended websites:

www.healthyaging.net

www.stitch.net

www.sixtyandme.com

www.projectrenewment.com

www.encore.org

www.aarp.com

CHAPTER NINE

1. Kathy Gottberg. "9 Reasons Why What You Think about Aging Matters" 11/14/2005 , Huffington Post. www.huffingtonpost.com

2. Laura Robbins. "The Pernicious Problem of Ageism" 10/22/2015 ASA Generations Journal of the American Society on Aging www.asaging.org

3. www.scambusters.org

CHAPTER TEN

1. Alzheimer's Association (www.alz.org)

2. Dr. Gary Small and Gigi Vorgan , *2 Weeks to Younger Brain,* (West Palm Beach, Humanix Books, 2015)

3. Dr. Mark Hyman, "Alzherimer's = Type 3 diabetes, February 16, 2016. www.drhyman.com

4. Dr. Fred Gage "Neurogenesis in the Adult Brain" Salk Institute for Biological Sudies, retrieved March 21, 2016, www.logg.salk.edu

5. Dr. Brant Cortright, *The Neurogenesis Diet &Lifestyle; Upgrade Your Brain, Upgrade Your Life.* (Mill Valley, Psyche ,Media, 2015)

6. Dr. Amen. www.danielamenmd.com

7. Dr. Monique Giroux "Neuroplasticity/Brain Smart Living =with Dr. Giroux". Retrived 3/21/2016. www.drgiroux.xom/neuroplasticity/

CHAPTER ELEVEN

1. Dr. Brian Weatherdon. Notes from phone interview, March 15, 2016.

   Website: www.guaranteedincomeforlife.ca

2. Dr. Siamak N Nabili "Advance Medical Directives (Living Will, Power of Attorney and Health-Care Proxy)" Retrieved March 22nd, 2016. www.medicinenet.com

CPSIA information can be obtained
at www.ICGtesting.com
Printed in the USA
LVOW01s1836200217

524831LV00028B/1708/P